Thomas Hay Sweet Escott

A Trip to Paradoxia and Other Humours of the Hour

Being contemporary pictures of social fact and political fiction

Thomas Hay Sweet Escott

A Trip to Paradoxia and Other Humours of the Hour
Being contemporary pictures of social fact and political fiction

ISBN/EAN: 9783337068530

Printed in Europe, USA, Canada, Australia, Japan

Cover: Foto ©Suzi / pixelio.de

More available books at **www.hansebooks.com**

A TRIP TO PARADOXIA

AND OTHER HUMOURS OF THE HOUR

Being Contemporary Pictures of Social Fact and Political Fiction

BY

T. H. S. ESCOTT

Author of "Personal Forces of the Period."
"Platform, Press, Politics, and Play."
"The Social Transformation of the Victorian Age."
"England : Its People, Polity, and Pursuits."

LONDON
GREENING & CO.
20 CECIL COURT, CHARING CROSS ROAD

1899

DEDICATORY

SOME of the sketches in this little book were suggested by chance words of witty wisdom from the lips of Mr. Gladstone's successor in the Premiership. The volume is therefore inscribed to

THE EARL OF ROSEBERY, K.G.,

with all thanks for the kindness and encouragement shown during many years to the writer's industry. With that name I may be permitted in the inscription to include that of Stanhope, whose noble house has by different members of it shown an interest in the writer; of Sir William and Lady Priestley, as well as of my two oldest and kindest friends in literary London, Clement Scott and Joseph Knight. These two last have by their friendly interest, renewed after many years from our first acquaintance, cheered the weariness of physical convalescence after illness, and so ministered to health.

T. H. S. ESCOTT.

PREFATORY

THE very slight sketches, that scarcely pretend to be tales, of which this small volume consists, apart from the relations of time in which the later stands to the earlier work, have some connection with earlier works by the present writer. *England,* etc. (Cassell, 2 vols. ; Chapman and Hall, 1 vol.), was a survey of English institutions actually at work. *Social Transformations* (Seeley) brought down that book to the present day. *Personal Forces* (Hurst and Blackett) was an attempt to show the influence on their age of certain well-known individuals. The present sketches show in outline certain of the fashions or the humours of the period, themselves the products partly of our polity, partly of those who live under it.

T. H. S. E.

BRIGHTON, 1899.

TWELVE
CLEVER AND POPULAR
NOVELS

THE HYPOCRITE.
Third Edition. 2s. 6d.

THE GREEN PASSION.
By ANTHONY P. VERT. 3s. 6d.

A SOCIAL UPHEAVAL.
By ISIDORE G. ASCHER. 6s.

THE SWORD OF FATE.
By HENRY HERMAN. 3s. 6d.

SEVEN NIGHTS WITH SATAN.
By J. L. OWEN. 3s. 6d.

LORD JIMMY.
By GEORGE MARTYN. 2s. 6d.

FAME THE FIDDLER.
By S. J. ADAIR FITZ-GERALD. 2s. 6d.

THE RESURRECTION OF HIS GRACE.
By CAMPBELL RAE-BROWN. 2s. 6d.

THE GATES OF TEMPTATION.
By Mrs. ALBERT S. BRADSHAW. 2s. 6d.

THE DOLOMITE CAVE.
By W. PATRICK KELLY. 3s. 6d.

THE LADY OF THE LEOPARD.
By CHAS. L'EPINE. 3s. 6d.

THE DEVIL IN A DOMINO.
By CHAS. L'EPINE. 1s.

CONTENTS

A TRIP TO PARADOXIA

I.

THE steamer having advanced half-way up the estuary, was now approaching the chief port of the great kingdom of Paradoxia. The shore, instead of being lined with palaces, as one of the two passengers in whom we are interested had expected, displayed an unpicturesque fringe of rather squalid dwellings, or of very smoke-begrimed factories.

Observing a look of surprise on the face of Kalogathus, an entire stranger from the neighbouring country of Hilaria, now visiting Dumdum, the Paradoxian capital, for the first time, his companion and cicerone, one Glybbe, a Paradoxian native of experience and position, anticipated the coming question by the remark, "You must know the Paradoxians are the most humble-minded people in the world, and do not live to astonish strangers with the magnificence of their city, therefore they show you at first all that is most poverty-stricken and least lovely."

Arrived at the landing-stage, Kalogathus observed that no policemen or other state guardians of public order were in sight.

"The fact is," responded his friend, "we do not need them, for the Paradoxians are notoriously the best-conducted people in the world."

The words had scarcely been uttered when two men of particularly villainous aspect, and obviously not quite sober, boarded the vessel, and engaged in a struggle for the custody of the visitors' chattels and person. During the confusion that followed, the hat of Kalogathus, an entirely new creation of the most expert and expensive Hilarian artist, was knocked off his head, crushed beneath his feet, and finally thrown into the water. Being about to express dissatisfaction at his loss his friend checked him immediately, and putting his finger to his lips, observed, "Not a word. I protest the man was very sorry for it, and, if you give him sixpence, will very likely say no more about it, for all the Paradoxians are politeness itself."

When he had struggled through the gangway to the shore Kalogathus discovered that his watch was gone.

"It is really of no consequence," rejoined Glybbe, "there are more clocks in Dumdum than in any other capital under the sun, and as for your property, I saw the man take it out of your pocket, and should not be at all surprised if, when you get to your hotel, he offered to let you have it again for a ten-pound note; the truth is, you Hilarians have

no idea of the honesty of us simple Dumdumites."

As there were no conveyances of any
kind in sight, Kalogathus meekly inquired
how he was to get to his first destination.
His companion seemed grieved and hurt
by the question. "Is it possible?" he
exclaimed, "that you, who have been
reading the daily paper all the way, did
not know that the Dumdum cabdrivers had
all struck?"

On being asked what a cab-strike might
mean, Glybbe responded, "The working
men of Paradoxia, you must know, are a
practical people, and when they have nothing in their pockets leave their wives
and children to get on as best they may,
and fastening a big card on their coats,
printed with the words 'WE ARE STARVING,'
adjourn to the next public-house till it is
the hour to go to the theatre."

"And," innocently commented Kalo -

gathus, "does this put the money they want in their pockets?"

At this point the born citizen of the most practical country in the world fairly lost his patience.

"Have you Hilarians," he broke out almost angrily, "no idea of the brotherhood of mankind, or of the rights of labour and the sanctity of Trades Unions? But see, here is my own private victoria, and in ten minutes you will be at home."

They had not gone far when Kalogathus noticed from the carriage a man mercilessly beating a pale-faced woman, while two ragged children, terror-stricken, stood by. Being a person of humane impulses, and observing none of the bystanders were disposed to interfere, Kalogathus was about to descend to make the cowardly brute desist.

"Do nothing of the sort," appealingly murmured Glybbe, "or they will both turn and rend you; surely you must be aware that Paradoxians are domesticated to a proverb, and would go to the stake for the inviolability of their home."

"But the poor woman and the helpless infants," continued Kalogathus. "What are they to do?"

"They will all make it up presently," quickly explained his friend, "and go together to Bounderby Gardens to spend a happy day. Bless you, my friend," he continued, "it is only their play, and you will have to stay some time in Paradoxia before you know what a humorous people we are."

Arrived at a fine street in a fashionable precinct, consisting, as it seemed, chiefly of hotels, the Paradoxian delivered the stranger to the manager of one of these caravanserais, and, whispering something into that functionary's ear, told Kalogathus he would find the charges moderate, and promised to call upon him to-morrow. As, however, it was by this time quite plain to the Hilarian visitor that words used in common by his friend and himself had not precisely the same meaning, he took the precaution of inquiring the cost of the two conveniently furnished apartments to which he had been shown.

"A mere bagatelle, my dear sir, I assure you," replied the hotel manager, flipping a fly off his highly-polished boots, "only £25 a week, not, of course, including bath or lights; but the reason we can let you have it so cheap is that Prince Rumpelstiltskin, the Baratarian Ambassador, had to leave hurriedly to-day, and at the end of the season we Dumdumites always lower our charges."

Having performed a mental calculation, and found that the annual cost of this domicile would considerably exceed the salary of the Prime Minister in his own country, Kalogathus rang the bell with a view of ordering his baggage to be transferred elsewhere. Instead of the waiter the rival proprietor of a neighbouring establishment rushed into the apartment, and, being informed of the stranger's difficulty, at once offered to provide him with superior accommodation for rather less than half the sum. Before the bargain was concluded an emissary from yet another joint-stock palace for distinguished strangers, to whom it had been rumoured incorrectly that Kalogathus was the special correspondent of the chief Hilarian newspaper, breathlessly entered, and drawing our friend into a little private closet, whispered in his ear that he would be proud and pleased to entertain him royally as long as he liked, and make no charge for lodging but only for board. Struck by the liberality of the arrangement, Kalogathus had hardly given the order for the removal when a magnificent lackey, with the words blazoned on his gold hat-band "Royal Empire Residential Club," opening the door and laying his hand upon the newcomer's shoulder, told him with a stately bow that beneath his roof Kalogathus should not only have rent free an apartment worthy of his rank, but that venison, grouse, turtle, all the delicacies of the season, and dry champagne of a famous brand, should gratuitously grace his board.

Not quite liking the idea of eleemosynary hospitality, and anxious to find repose somewhere before, Actæon-like, he should be rent in pieces by competitive innkeepers, Kalogathus made his escape, bundled all his goods into a four-wheeled fly, and drove afar from this magnificent quarter to a quite unfashionable and somewhat dingy precinct, where he remembered to have read comfortable lodgings were to be found with the good old Paradoxian fare at moderate charges.

Reaching his destination without further misadventure, he subsided into rump-steak and oyster sauce with a pint of stout in the coffee-room, and ten minutes afterwards was snoring virtuously between the sheets.

"What a swindler that first hotel-keeper was," next morning remarked Kalogathus to his friend when he called upon him, "for wanting to charge me at the rate of £1300 a year for what another would let me have for half the price, another for nothing at all, and a third not only for nothing, but with venison and champagne thrown in."

"I perceive," replied Glybbe, "that as yet you understand imperfectly the use of our language. There has been no swindle in the matter—the first rooms at £25 a week were cheap enough ; as for the second offer, it is what they always make, and the only reason why they do not lose money in the long run is because their terms enable them to do such a big business."

Kalogathus being of a logical turn of mind, and not quite following the argument, was about to ask a question, but politely fearing it might be inconvenient, checked himself, when his friend continued: "As you get to know more of Dumdum and Paradoxia, you will see that the great social feature of the century has been hotel enterprise. But come, it is now time to be getting on, as I wish you to see as much as possible of our national life in all its departments; and first let us go to the 'Assembly of the Silent,' also known as the manufactory of statute law, of which I myself have the honour to be a member. This body is, as doubtless you know, the great depository of all power, and the real centre of government in Paradoxia."

Kalogathus, who thought that, by contrast with his native official-ridden Hilaria, he had seen as yet no traces of authority in Paradoxia, could not help remarking, "That explains, then, why your government in this country is so confoundedly bad."

Jeremiah Glybbe, Esq., a puffy little man with a red face, and swelling with a sense of his own legislative dignity, drawing himself up to his full height, which was at least five feet four inches, and throwing the strongest look he could command of wounded and contemptuous dignity into his rather podgy and expressionless features, told his friend in rejoinder that he "ought to keep silence on these matters till he knew more about them," and that practically the Paradoxians in general, and the Dumdumites in particular, were acknowledged to be the best-governed people in the world. On their drive towards their next object of interest, during which the admirable control over the traffic in the Dumdum streets caused them to sustain only two serious accidents, Glybbe explained to his guest that the title, "The Assembly of the

Silent," was a facetious euphemism, seeing that the only member of it ever known to hold his tongue was an official, who was, of course, called "The Orator," and who was paid a handsome salary to coerce others into the doing of that which he was not allowed to do himself.

"I suppose," groaned Kalogathus to himself, after receiving this information, "I shall gradually get to understand the remarkable use made by these people of their mother-tongue."

Once inside the precincts, before they had actually entered the Chamber itself, the scene rather reminded the visitor of a country fair in his native land than suggested any association with State business. In one corner of the stately vestibule was a refreshment booth, at which two rather wild-eyed and unkempt gentlemen seemed to be regaling themselves on a roast potato and a bottle of gingerbeer. These personages, who talked a dialect of the Parodoxian language with which even Glybbe confessed himself imperfectly acquainted, and who illustrated their remarks by a variety of gestures rather after the Hilarian than the Paradoxian pattern, were, it seemed, Blarnian members of the Silent Assembly, who, passing most of their days and nights within these walls to save the cost of lodging, presently proceeded to a secluded nook, and producing a pocket comb and looking‑glass, went on to complete their morning's toilette.

"I have read," mildly observed the some‑what surprised Kalogathus to his cicerone, "that in Blarnia they distil a spirit from cauliflower so powerful as to take two men to carry off a small glass of it. If we were to ask that gentleman, perhaps he would kindly give me a few drops of it to wash down this hard-boiled egg, for I feel rather faint."

As he gasped out these words his friend

kicked his unoffending shin as an admoni-
tion to silence, and having observed that,
had the Blarnian patriots overheard the allu-
sion to the native beverage they would certainly have claimed his blood, asked poor
Kalogathus if he had not noticed a piece
of white metal, about the size of a cartwheel, tied by a ribbon as broad as a
hat-band round the necks of the two
gentlemen in question. On asking what
might be the meaning of that which he
could scarcely fail to see, our stranger was
told that it proved the wearers of the
decoration never to take anything stronger
than water.

"Is, then," Kalogathus burst forth in
surprise, "drunkenness so universal in your
country that everybody who is content with
stale buns and gingerbeer proclaims the
fact by dressing himself in that grotesque
fashion?"

"My good friend," rejoined Glybbe,

"please remember you are in a public place, and don't ask such rude questions. In a little time you will know that these gentlemen consider it their duty to encourage the others."

It was, however, as Glybbe, in the official phrase of Paradoxia, was "free to admit," somewhat unfortunate that his guest's visit should occur when the time of the Assembly was entirely monopolized by the great Blarnian question.

"My dear Glybbe," remarked the visitor, "I have read your newspapers for nearly half a century, and I can never recall a day when there was not a Blarnian question."

Taking no notice of this comment, Glybbe conducted Kalogathus to a place in the gallery inside the Assembly-room, and bidding him to order for his refreshment any luxuries of the season, such as pineapple-drops or whelks, hurried away to take his part in the business of legislation below. The

Paradoxians being the most practical people in the world, it did not surprise Kalogathus to learn from his next-door neighbour that the chamber on which he was now looking down was constructed on such principles and dimensions as not to contain a third of those entitled to sit in it, that the competition for places was the cause of periodical revolutions, and the struggles for seats between its members the occasion of sanguinary frays.

"Perhaps," timidly soliloquized Kalogathus, "these very practical people might get on better if they were a little more theoretical."

Amid the babel of confused sounds and inarticulate clamour beneath and in front of him, Kalogathus for some time could only distinguish isolated words, chiefly proper names, and occasional syllables, mostly significant of reproach or vituperation, taken from the sacred books of the Paradoxian people, who were, of course,

ç

the most religious in the world. In the midst of the excitement, which every moment grew fiercer and noisier, Kalogathus presently recognized his acquaintance of the cartwheel and blue ribbon waving a stout ashen cudgel above his head, and, to show, as Kalogathus supposed, his own humility, inviting anyone who liked to tread on the tail of his coat, a generous offer that did not, if accepted, seem likely to take any gloss of novelty off that garment. Presently this particular Blarnian patriot provoked a fiercer fray, and, wildly making for a gentleman on an opposite bench, after having begun seemingly to twist his head from his shoulders, hurled his unresisting form full length upon the floor. The *mêlée* now became general and wilder; blood flowed; eyes were blackened; the imprecatory vocabulary of the Paradoxian language, which is not of narrow compass, began to be exhausted; and the arena presented a series of hand-to-hand battles like those that make up the sum of warfare of the *Iliad.* Kalogathus, a grateful guest, began to be frightened for the fate of his conductor and host, but was immensely relieved when he saw him safely outside the limits of the fray, peacefully taking a cup of tea and a muffin on the steps of the President's chair. The wretched Kalogathus, who had swallowed no substantial food since his steak and stout on the preceding night, began to be aware internally of the vacuum proverbially abhorred by nature, but was at this moment rejoined by Glybbe, whose arm he now perceived to be in a sling. " Perhaps," said that gentleman to his half-famished friend, " we might now find ourselves a pint of claret and a cutlet in the dining-room."

While they were moving thitherwards Kalogathus observed one of the officials, as the Chamber was now empty, quietly proceeding to remove all signs of the recent excitement, brushing up a few broken limbs, carefully removing all crimson stains, and handing over a brace of Blarnian belligerents, insatiable of battle, to functionaries whose care it was to conduct them to the place of safe seclusion reserved for Blarnian patriots overpowered by the lust of strife.

While they were seated at their repast the Paradoxian legislator brushed the incident aside as one of no importance, but the House's passions, he admitted, were so heated that it really seemed at one time as if something might happen. However, the legislation which had provoked all this was now fairly disposed of, and nothing more was wanted than the ratification of the Crimson Tippets, by which he meant another section of the Paradoxian manufacturers of statute law.

" I suppose," eagerly interrupted Kalogathus, " it is a mere matter of form?"

"That," responded Glybbe, "is by no means the case; you seem to forget that we Paradoxians are a practical people, and the State does not pay Crimson Tippets to do nothing. Our House has been working for three months at this business, and now to-morrow the Crimson Tippets will begin to undo all we have done in three days."

"What an absurdity!" was the exclamation that Kalogathus could not repress.

"My dear friend," was the other's gentle rebuke, "you really should not criticise where you don't understand. This is not absurdity; it is what the greatest of our statesmen calls 'the free play of the Constitution.'

"By-the-bye," he added, "there is to be to-morrow in the Great Amphitheatre a demonstration against the Crimson Tippets." Observing a look of perplexity on his companion's face, Glybbe added, "A demonstration, you should know, is so called because it demonstrates nothing, except that if the weather is fine more people than usual will be prevented from enjoying it in our recreation grounds."

The event thus referred to by Glybbe was duly witnessed a few days later by the two friends. A brass band preceded the demonstrationists through the streets, till at last not less than three-score of souls, infants in arms included, were marshalled round a stunted ash tree in a picturesque meadow on the outskirts of Dumdum. Mr. Harmodius Flam, a colleague of Glybbe in the Assembly of the Silent, and also the conductor of the *Down with Everything* newspaper, informed the visitor to Paradoxia, when they met him a few moments later, that he saw before him the great Paradoxian people assembled in the majesty of their millions, and that to-morrow there was not a Crimson Tippet in the empire who would fail to tremble at the report of

the historic event. Kalogathus was about
to ask another of his inconvenient questions,
when the man of ink and scissors observed
that he had an appointment to lunch with,
as struck Kalogathus, curiously enough, one
of those very Crimson Tippets whom Mr.
Flam, in his newspaper, denounced as the
arch-miscreants of the universe.

II.

Some little time subsequently, in com-
pliance with his visitor's request for information on the political system of
Paradoxia, Glybbe expressed himself to
Kalogathus after this manner. Apropos
of the Hilarian's surprise at the variety
of Paradoxian parties, the well-informed
resident said :—

"As a matter of fact, we have in
Paradoxia fewer political parties than in
any other country in the world, and you

must know, my dear Kalogathus, that in all States these are the same in reality and in purpose, if not in number, and a better clue to them is less a history-book than a grammar. 'I want,' 'you have,' 'I will get' —decline these verbs, and apply them with the necessary changes to all communities, and you have an exhaustive exposition of the party system. Here we talk of pro- and anti - Blarnians, of Crimson and of anti-Crimson Tippetites, but in Paradoxia, as elsewhere, there are only two divisions of any real account—the 'haves' and the 'have nots.' These are eternal."

"I had heard," mildly interpolated Kalogathus, "much about the confusion and decay of the Paradoxian party system."

"That," quickly replied Glybbe, "is the consequence of our leaders having ceased to be statesmen and become auctioneers. Our guerilla chiefs to-day pretend to rally a following which is non - existent for a policy which is unreal. Only once let our great men find out what the people really want, then combine to supply or deny that need, as the case may be, and you may be quite sure, my good Kalogathus, you will hear no more pessimistic platitudes like these. As for the question of the hour, look at that man yonder ; he is the question of the hour."

The individual thus referred to was engaged outside in cleaning the windows of the apartment where they were sitting. He had now been nearly eighty minutes at work, and had not yet fully finished a single pane of glass. After having polished a couple of square inches he would complacently survey the result of his labour, refresh himself from a little stone jar in his pocket, or, lighting his pipe, would moodily growl forth, "Cruel work, I call it," and then make a feeble show of resuming his labours.

"That man," said Glybbe, "has a wife and children waiting for bread in the river-side garret which he calls his home. He could do easily in thirty minutes what he now spreads over an hour, and could without trouble make five shillings for every three that his employers pay him to-day."

"Is he, then," broke in the astonished Kalogathus, "a gentleman of fortune disguised as an artisan in a smock?"

"On the contrary," was the reply, "he belongs to a company of men who make their bread by the sweat of their brow, but who would cause his life to be not worth a week's purchase if he proceeded at all less leisurely than he is now doing. That is the difficulty we have here to solve. The whole fabric of Paradoxian industry rests upon a basis of free labour, and free it cannot be if it is regulated by the class bullies who call themselves 'representative working men.' The worst is that this sort of thing makes honest labour the least welcome to those for whom it is the most necessary. Having long furnished the example of a race of toilers, we are incurring the reproach of a race of shirkers, so that the pith and purpose, the nerve and pluck of the Paradoxian people, itself the product of labour, are being destroyed."

"And the remedy?" inquired Kalogathus.

"The restoration of duty to the place which it used to hold among us," replied Glybbe.

"Your religion," soliloquized, half aloud, Kalogathus, "ought, I should think, to help you here."

On hearing this Glybbe became visibly thoughtful, and even dejected. It had indeed for some time been noticeable that the blithe and even chirpy optimism which reflected his nature in his manner was becoming overcast by the influences of his friend's rather unwelcome conversation and often painfully inconvenient inquiries. The truth is, contact with a stranger had given a new turn to this gentleman's reflections, and raised unpleasant doubts in his mind whether the conventional praises heaped upon the Paradoxian polity in all its departments were at bottom deserved by the facts, or whether he, like many of his excellent and amiable countrymen, might not unconsciously have been living in a "paradise of fools" and an Elysium of hypocrites. Instead, therefore, of replying with his usual alacrity to the invitation of Kalogathus to enter upon a fresh theme, Glybbe muttered something about this being really quite out of his line, and that the best thing for Kalogathus to do would be to summon a conference of Paradoxian divines. The stranger from Hilaria, therefore, good-humouredly gave the conversation a fresh turn, but, as he was travelling for information, did not abandon his quest, and took the opportunity in another quarter of

examining the religious condition of Paradoxia, and, through the help of duly-qualified
spiritual guides, eventually arrived at the
following results.

III.

That Paradoxia was the most religious
country in the world, and Dumdum among
its most devotional capitals, was generally
maintained and circumstantially demonstrated on all sides. When Kalogathus
intimated that he had heard the Paradoxians
credited by some of his own epicurean
compatriots with possessing a score of
religions, but a single sauce, he was rebuked
for the levity of his remark. As a matter
of fact, it was made plain to him that
in the spiritual, like the political, domain,
however innumerable the contending sects
and their subdivisions might be, there were
practically in Paradoxia only two great
schools. The faith of the community had

been changed more than once by the decree
of the Silent Assembly, and its ceremonial
displays were the periodical subjects of
frequent legislation, but now, as ever, the
real and only issue was between those who
held and those who denied that the Divine
Being had made a manifestation of Himself
and of His will to men.   Among the deniers
persuasion there were, strange as it may
seem, some of the most ostentatiously pious
and aggressively devout members of the
Paradoxian Church.

Professor Nephelos, an erudite doctor in
the chief university of the realm, had
demonstrated to his own satisfaction, and
to the great pain of his more humble-
minded disciples, that the realities indicated
to the Creator's judgment by the epithets
good, bad, just, unjust, merciful, and so
forth, were utterly beyond the power of a
human mind to grasp, or even to conjecture, and that consequently one could not

be perfectly sure that superhuman codes of morality might not, in effect, enjoin the exact opposite of those things which to the human ear and intelligence they seemed to command. When, somewhat staggered by this proposition, Kalogathus mildly protested that its tendency must be to drive ordinary persons into the most revolting extremes of immorality and atheism, he was abruptly told by a very superior academic that if he understood the doctrine of the Relativity of Knowledge better he would not make such ridiculous remarks. The more deeply, however, Kalogathus mused over the matter the more unconvinced he became, nor was he sorry to find that some of the most blameless and beneficent members of the Paradoxian community shared and profoundly sympathized with his views.

"We have here," remarked one of these gentlemen to him, "yet to decide whether the Highest Object of all reverence and fear is a beneficent or a maleficent Being, and until we desist from contemplating Him through false media, because through the mists of Professor Nephelos, we shall not have reached the very threshold of Truth.   These metaphysics run mad it is which constitutes the real enemy of a healing faith in the traditionally religious realm of Paradoxia.   The nominal division," the present speaker continued, " may be between the two rival sects who claim to have the power of working a certain miracle ; but the vital and only actively real difference is that separating those who assert from those who specifically, or virtually, deny that the Great Architect of the visible world has placed, and is prepared to gratify, in His creatures the desire and power of faintly understanding His attri- butes — has given them the faculties of thought and language, has implanted in

them rudimentary ideas of ethics, not for
the purpose of mocking or tormenting
them, but for their own well-being, happiness, and guidance here. Many of those
who admit theoretically that this is so,
practically in some of their sects dis-
allow it. Sometimes they say that by the
immutable order of the universe, the right
apprehension of these high matters is the
exclusive business of a caste; sometimes,
as by the sectarian opponents of these
individuals, one is told that all will be
clear if we listen to 'the still small voice'
of a divinely-nurtured faith."

"And," inquired Kalogathus, "what does
'faith' mean?"

"Faith," resumed his acquaintance very
slowly and sadly, "as used by some teachers
of ours, means, I regret to say, the professing to believe what all the analogies of
existence, all received ideas of good and
evil, all social moralities, the very structure
D

of the human mind itself, tell one must be untrue, and the professing to adore and love a Being who is represented by those who claim to be His exclusive votaries as the concentration and essence of the very qualities which most revolt human hearts and most revolt human affections. Some few centuries ago we in Paradoxia spent much blood and treasure to shake off the tyranny which froze the heart and paralyzed the sentiment, and to establish once for all the supreme verity that the sanctions of morality and religion must in all cases be identical, and not contradictory. I regret to have to admit," he added, "that the victory we thought we had gained was superficial and evanescent, and that to-day a war, deadlier perhaps to all which is best in our national life and ideals than the old one, is being waged between the religion-ists, who should rather be called the anti-nomians, and the enemies of anti-nomianism, who, seeing that they are the friends of morality, are those who alone can be called religious.

A little further experience and conversation with those who had replaced the original message from the invisible world by the garbled narrative of it from a foreign capital, subsequently showed to Kalogathus the meaning of these observations; and that amiable inquirer saw with real grief that the bitterest enemies of peace and goodwill on earth were the descendants of the very champions who several generations earlier, in the organic struggle referred to by Glybbe, had held aloft the flag of emancipation from human control. One of these apologists endeavoured seriously to convince Kalogathus that reverent devotion to the order of the invisible world necessarily implied continual malice and uncharitableness to certain members of the seen creation.

"For," he went on explanatorily, "it is my first duty to hate all that is evil. Now, how can I fail to see that my fellow-beings generally are evil? Personally I am a water-drinker. I have outlived the period of the passions. I am the father of fourteen children; my life is, therefore, one of great austerity. On the other hand, I admit I am mean, unconscionably shabby, and not, according to human standards, too honest or truthful; but what of that? It is my paramount duty to signalize my hatred of those sins to which I myself for social and physiological reasons am not inclined. I therefore horsewhipped my wife last night because of a remark I disapproved, and shut my door upon my prodigal son because he had about him a decided aroma of cigars and brandy-and-water. In this present state of being we are so fashioned that we cannot hate the evil without hating the evil-doer. Pity for the sinner would imply condonation of the sin ; therefore it is my first obligation to hate sin and sinner alike indiscriminately, and to do what I can to crush them both. And now, Mr. Kalogathus," concluded this exemplary pietist somewhat tartly, "I hope you are satisfied."

But Kalogathus, who had himself dipped into the sacred writings of the Paradoxians, meekly expostulated that he did not quite see it.

"That," replied this admirable person, who happened to be a grocer in good business, "is because you are delivered over to judicial blindness, and are, I much fear, an emissary of evil ; but now I must leave you, for I have to apply the birch-rod to my youngest child for telling a 'fib,' and after that it will be time to punish the apprentice and then talk about charities."

After this conversation Kalogathus was disposed to feel less surprised than he was before at the disagreeable condition of the

public streets and squalid courts in certain
parts of the great capital of Dumdum ; but
the great festival of the illustrious college
of Cloud Compellers was approaching, and
before attending this our visitor thought he
might as well relax his mind by mixing in
the more modish society in Dumdum, to the
chief leaders of which letters of introduction
were lying at his hotel.

IV.

Mrs. Lightinhand was at once one of the
leading hostesses in Dumdum society and
one of the most accomplished and ubiquitous
representatives of the tolerant cosmopolitan
eclectic, comprehensive yet discriminating,
spirit of her age. Kalogathus, she knew,
bore in his native land an excellent character
and had a modest competence, but she
would have welcomed him to her hospitable
and daintily-equipped home if he had been

supported by public subscriptions and was
without a shred of character for his back.
Being thoughtfully anxious to contribute his
quota to the conversational fund of amusement and instruction, our friend, on entering
the drawing-room and approaching a little
group which his hostess had formed round
her, was about to expatiate on his experi-
ences and to ask some of his usual questions.
Just then a gentleman of very remarkable
aspect, whose intellect had made him famous
equally in society and in the State, came up,
and on being asked by Mrs. Lightinhand to
give a few words of advice to her little boys,
then seated side by side upon the couch, and
about to return to school the next day, went
up to them and, as Kalogathus thought,
with a rather sardonic smile, while pleasantly patting the head of the elder brother,
said, " When you go out into the world, my
little fellow, be sure never to ask 'Who was
the man with the iron mask ? ' or they will

call you a bore; and you, my boy," he continued, turning to the other, "never want to know 'Who wrote the letters of Junius?' or they will call you a bigger bore than your brother."

Kalogathus could not, had he wished, have helped overhearing the words, and it struck him that they might be politely intended for him. Be that as it may, our stranger met with slight encouragement to persevere in his attempts in the drawing-room to make himself agreeable. His comments and inquiries alike fell upon heedless listeners, while the ladies and gentlemen about him persisted uninter-ruptedly in a conversation charged with allusions he could not understand to persons of whom he had never heard, and spiced with an *argot* the interpretation of which he could only conjecture vaguely from the context.

It was the same kind of thing throughout

the excellent dinner provided by Mrs. Lightinhand for her guests. When the ladies
had withdrawn and coffee was served, a
pale-faced youth, producing a thing in
Britannia metal called by him a cigarette-
box, and offering one of its contents to
Kalogathus, ventured to condole with our
friend on being, in the pallid stripling's
phrase, "rather out of it."

"If," was our friend's reply, "this sort of
talk had been going on in my country, it
would have been considered very provincial."

Here the guest who in the drawing-room
had spoken so encouragingly to Mrs. Lightinhand's little sons interposed as follows :—

"The more you see of us, my good sir,
the more you will find out that 'smart'
society and provincialism are only different
names for the same thing. This moment
at every dinner-table throughout the fashionable quarter of Dumdum, in every castle, in
every cottage, in every club, and in every

village tavern up and down the land, the great Paradoxian people are amusing themselves with the same allusive small talk and gossip about those things which are part of their own lives, and which have no interest to any other creatures except themselves, for the very good reason that they have no meaning. The longer you dine out in Dumdum the less you will find there is of general conversation. If the company is large it chatters in groups and libels its neighbours in detachments. These coteries coalesce as little with each other as if they were in separate rooms or towns. The different currents of gabble never converge in one common stream of friendly intercourse."

"And yet," observed Kalogathus, "the Paradoxians are the most social people in the world."

"No doubt of that," said the other. "We carry the idea of joint-stock enterprise into all that we do or see or visit. We make parties for the play, we visit the hovels of the poor in detachments, and even our acts of devotion we perform in battalions, and yet," he added, "there is no country in the world where there is less real companionship at the present moment than Paradoxia."

On regaining the drawing-room, the appearance of two gentlemen at once strongly arrested the gaze of Kalogathus. The first of these was a personage arrayed in the ordinary evening dress of the country, but with a shock head of tangled hair, innocent of the brush, light in colour, and silken in texture, though so rudely tumbled that this part of his person might have been imported from the neighbouring isle of Blarnia. Standing by him was a little gentleman with smooth face, amiable but rather heavy eyes, habited in a short, tailless, black velvet sack, his nether limbs encased in trunk hose of crimson silk, while his linen, instead of being starched in the ordinary Paradoxian fashion, blossomed forth into a voluptuous wealth of muslin puffs and frills. From the evident awe with which the companion of this creature inspired the other occupants of the room, and the deferential air that some of them displayed on being presented to him, Kalogathus inferred that he was a person of high distinction. His features had been disciplined to express a super-cilious unconsciousness of all that was said and done around him. When spoken to he either remained stolidly silent or bluntly contradicted any statement from anybody that happened to reach his ears.

"Who," whispered Kalogathus to his next-door neighbour, "is that insufferable brute?"

"Great powers!" was the reply *sotto voce*, "he is the Duke of Z——, and the great leader of the Crimson Tippets."

"In Hilaria," Kalogathus ventured to

comment, "he would have to fight two duels before breakfast to-morrow."

"In Paradoxia," was the rejoinder, "if he was not a Crimson Tippet and a duke he would have been ducked in the first horse-pond long before now."

The younger gentleman turned out to be Mr. Euphues Twang, the poet of the season, discovered by Mrs. Lightinhand for the de-lectation of Dumdum. At this moment he was trying to secure the ear of his disdainful companion to his instructive comments on the "too utterly utter," or "too distinctly precious," as illustrated in the salons and picture galleries of the year. The duke resignedly bore it as long as he could, and not till he had yawned audibly half a dozen times, and twice had even begun to doze, did he, shaking himself together like a great Newfoundland dog, find that he had an appointment at the chamber of Crimson Tippets, and vanish into the night and

the recesses of his own brougham outside.
Ten minutes after he had left his political
business with the Crimson Tippets the
duke was whirling in a night express to
the provincial town of Oldcastle, where he
kept his racing stud, and the next morning
early Kalogathus saw him, costumed exactly
as if he had been a groom, riding for his
health's sake on the "Amazons' Promenade,"
as the chief equestrian resort in Dumdum is
called.

"The fashions of dress in this place,"
a few days later observed to a friend Kalogathus, while watching the motley crowd in
the neighbourhood of the "sacred promenade," "amuse me vastly. Your infants in
their perambulators are clothed like old
women, your old women like girls in their
teens ; your men affect the effeminacy of
women, your women ape the jackets
and the masculineness of men ; your great
nobles out of the season and in the pro-

vinces are, to look at, as working-men, grooms, covert-beaters, gamekeepers, and so forth ; your artisans on holidays cannot be distinguished from the ministers of one of your temples."

"My dear Kalogathus," rejoined Glybbe, after listening to these remarks, "you are occupying your mind with sad frivolities, but next week I shall show you something more instructive and improving, for our Cloud Compellers, the national assembly of our wise men, meet in conference at Cuckoo Town, where you will both hear and see the great Professor Poldoodle and his famous ape."

v.

To make these observations and references clear, some explanation will be necessary. Many years before this a very learned Paradoxian, Professor Chang, after considerable research and many experiments involving much torture to unoffending animals, had convinced himself and scientific society generally, that the aboriginal and prehistoric man was the evolved descendant of a race of very respectable monkeys. This view held the field till, a new sensation being necessary, a rival savant, Professor Slime, made it as clear as mud that the archetypal and earliest human denizen of this earth was the first-begotten of a frog.

Avidly seized at the time, and fondly cherished for a considerable season, the tadpole theory of human existence was generally credited, till at a memorable meeting of the savants an inveterate opponent of Slime, to the astonishment of his audience, produced a remarkably well-grown specimen of the tribe of Ranæ, who, somewhat huskily but quite articulately, croaked forth an indignant disavowal of all human affinities. Waxing warm with tribal enthusiasm, this highly intelligent reptile protested against the imputation of any such degrading relationship ; for could there be any beings, except man, so igno- rant and so involved in self-conceit as to ignore the fact that the immemorially ancient race of Frogs were the lineal descendants of the mighty mammoth icthy- osaurus family, and were prosperously settled in Egypt long before any human biped fouled the waters of the Nile.

This declaration had the effect of once more popularizing the ape theory, on which, it was now significantly whispered, recent discoveries of Professor Poldoodle would throw a wholly novel and a surprisingly unexpected light. Poldoodle having, from his childish visits to the Zoological Gardens, conceived the idea that apes talked to them- selves, and might even be induced to talk to mankind, had lately gratified the ambition of his existence by passing a prolonged

E

holiday inside a comfortably fitted-up cage
in the depths of an Ethiopian forest, and at
a spot frequented by the most highly fashionable and cultured of Simian society.   Not
only had he satisfied himself by aural and
ocular observation from behind his bars
that apes hold habitually more improving
conversation than the inhabitants of Paradoxia, but he had succeeded in inducing one
of these bipeds to accompany him to his
home in the city of Dumdum, and, as was
said, to attend with him the great gathering
of Paradoxian Cloud Compellers at Cuckoo
Town.

When the eventful day came the largest
and most splendid building of Cuckoo Town
was crammed with representatives of whatever was most brilliant, cultivated, or wise
in Paradoxian society.   In a kind of amphitheatre on a raised daïs sat the great
Poldoodle, while beside him was a spacious
case or vessel covered with brown holland,

which, it was rumoured, contained the stranger from Ethiopia. After a few introductory remarks, apologizing on the plea of catarrh for any hoarseness of his *protégé*, the professor beckoned the Simian guest, apparelled in the academic dress of Cuckoo Town, to the table. Having astonished the company by calling for a glass of iced water, the ape proceeded with great composure to deliver its address. The Simian lecturer began by protesting to the ladies and gentlemen present that for his part he was entirely without prejudice against his human fellow-creatures, and assured them that if he had not been born an ape he should feel it an honour to become a man, but, he added in a quotation picked up obviously in the classic atmosphere of Cuckoo Town, "Amicus Socrates, amicus Plato, magis amica veritas," and therefore, speaking not only as the representative of intelligent apedom, whose official representative he was, but as a well-wisher to humanity, whom he had no wish unjustly to disown, he felt bound, in the interests of that truth itself to the pursuit of which the halls and towers of Cuckoo Town were consecrated, to assure his hearers that the theory of his respected friend, as he would call him, Professor Chang, was totally devoid of all foundation in fact.

Profound sensation, it is needless to say, followed this remarkable repudiation by the interesting Simian on behalf of his species of all share in the paternity of man. Mrs. Lightinhand requested Professor Poldoodle to bring him to her next " Thursday afternoon," and to induce him to lecture in her music-room in the same series as Archdeacon Marmoset and other dignitaries of the Church, as well as celebrities in science, literature, or art. Lady Emily Highfalutin called him a " dear creature," while her little girl presented him with two macaroons and a whole bag of gingerbread nuts.

The Duchess of —— said "she adored intellect, whether in man or brute, and felt sure nothing would delight his Grace more than to see him at luncheon at Dulverton House any day the accomplished creature liked to look in."

Mr. Sciolist Hum, who presided over the committee, suggested that the monkey should become an honorary member of the Pierian Club in Pall Mall. Mr. Shakespeare-Smith at once turned off an impromptu sonnet to him that appeared next week in the *Haymarket Journal*, written and edited chiefly by ladies of the very highest quality. Mr. E. G. W. Bolingbroke - Jones, the well-known pamphleteer, and also the chief literary impressario, as well as professional diner-out, in Dumdum, at once made a note to ask him to contribute an exhaustive paper, without any personality in it, to the

next number of the *Exclusive Review*, where
no poor devils of professional writers were
ever admitted, and the order of literary
precedence was regulated by the Heralds'
College.   A little later Kalogathus became
somewhat intimately acquainted with this
most intelligent and best bred of apes.
In fact, the two ultimately developed into
bosom friends and confidants.   " Daisy "
was the name by which the interesting
Simian—now, of course, a lion of the first
order—was spoken of in the social circles
he condescended to adorn.

" I do not know," was his observation
to the Hilarian visitor about this time,
"whether to be most amused by the inno-
cence or disgusted by the vanity of these
droll Paradoxians. The other day, wanting a
little exercise, I leapt up from my chair at the
Pierian Club, tied myself by my tail round
a chandelier, and did a little trapeze per-
formance on my own account.   A waiter

walked up, said I was disturbing the old
gentlemen reading their newspapers, and
begged me to come down. All this time
I could hear about me the buzz of gossip
and scandal so gross, false, and cowardly
that in the depths of my native forest the
talkers would have been hissed out of
society."

What had struck Kalogathus principally
was not so much the nonsense talked in the
upper circles of Paradoxian society, as the
fact that these ladies and gentlemen in the
presence of strangers showed their gracious-
ness by remaining obstinately dumb, or by
the parade of a dialect and of innuendoes
only intelligible to one of their own set.

VI.

But another great surprise was in store
for Paradoxian society, and for Kalogathus
as a temporary member of it. For some

years the pundits of Dumdum and the executive committee of the erudite Cloud Compellers had denounced, persecuted, and visited with every form of social ostracism anyone who might dare to express his agreement with the sacred writings of the Paradoxian people as to the number of days in which the existing order of the visible universe was evolved. Of late it had been whispered that extraordinary testimony would soon be forthcoming to the historic accuracy of the august narrative in the minutest detail. The facts were as follows. A new member of the Royal Paradoxian Stargazers had not only discovered a wholly unsuspected planet at a distance of some forty or fifty miles from the inhabited earth, but had invented and brought to bear upon it a telescope so powerful, that comparatively small objects could be discerned with the same ease as a lady's features through a lorgnette on the other side of the great

Dumdum opera-house. After several years of patient survey, this enterprising observer observed on the adjacent orb a series of huge obelisks engraved with strange-looking but perfectly well-defined characters. By applying to these a camera of unusual strength, some very fine photographic impressions of the monoliths and their records were through the instantaneous process obtained ; microscopic examination showed the records so brought down, so to speak, from the heaven itself to be composed in characters that soon were read by scientific experts without much difficulty. In about three months there was issued from the Cuckoo Town University press a transcription in the Paradoxian vernacular of the newly-found record. To the surprise of all, and to the special disgust of a chosen company of Paradoxian priests, who some months previously had shown in a volume of essays that this portion of the Paradoxian sacred writings was a myth, the results now brought to light verified that narrative at every point. Immediately the executive committee of Cloud Compellers changed their tone, discovered that genuine science had always favoured the hypothesis of the credibility of the sacred narrative, and requested permission from the State to burn alive anyone who dared to dissent from it.

" It would really seem to me," Kalogathus, apropos of all the business, ventured to remark to one of the wise men of Dumdum, "that your science is after all not so very scientific."

" Hush, my friend," gently replied the other, "this is only the morning, and we shall very likely read an official contradiction of it in the extra-special edition of to-night's *Celestial Post.*"

" I hope not," gravely observed Kalogathus.

"The newspaper proprietors of Dum-dum," was the rejoinder, "hope differently, because if there were no lies to contradict there would be no special editions to publish. By-the-bye," he continued, "I have been asked by my friend its editor whether you could not yourself find time to write something for the *Evening Oracle*, perhaps a leading article."

On Kalogathus appearing a little puzzled, his friend, who had had much experience as a Paradoxian journalist, reassured him.

"You will have no difficulty about it; the editor will give you your subject, and the rest will all follow as easy as lying, The leading article of the approved Dumdum type is simply an essay written in three paragraphs, never containing more than three ideas, and consisting of a series of identical propositions so worded as to avoid tautology and to conceal repetition."

Thus it happened that a few days later

than this Kalogathus found a "printer's devil" knocking at his door, and began a series of compositions which the editor of the *Oracle* obligingly approved.

VII.

The energetic visitor to the Paradoxian capital was, however, overtaxing his constitution, and soon began to experience unmistakable signs of nervous exhaustion.

"How about your Dumdum doctors, my dear Glybbe?" was the question asked of his original cicerone by the distinguished invalid.

"The medical faculty in the Paradoxian capital," was Glybbe's rather pompous reply, "is admittedly the best in the world. Before you consult our chief physician I will get my own pet leech to look at you."

Dr. Hippocrates Toad, the gentleman thus alluded to, a very soft-mannered person, who was rising rapidly into a fashionable practice, tapped our friend's chest with something resembling an auctioneer's hammer, inspected his throat, made him repeat the numbers 999 first rapidly, then slowly, looked at his eyes with something which reminded him of a magic lantern, applied an electric battery to his right leg's calf with such an effect that the patient, by an involuntary kick, was near knocking over the apparatus and assaulting its proprietor.

"Don't give way, my dear friend, to these foolish fancies. I have examined you ophthalmoscopically and in every way; all that you want is a little more to occupy your mind and a few of our dinners at the Sunflower Club. Dine with me there to-morrow, to meet the Duke of ——, and if you can get him to come, that very distinguished and charming stranger who we society people, as you know, have christened Monsieur FitzDaisy."

On recounting this interview to Glybbe, and expressing surprise at Dr. Toad's satisfactory report, Glybbe smiled and shook his head.

"You must know," he said, "my friend, that the Dumdum doctors, who are undoubtedly the best and greatest on the face of the earth, make it a practice only to tell their patients what it is plain they wish to be told. How else do you suppose," he continued, checking in the bud some objective utterance of Kalogathus, "that a man like Hippocrates Toad, who began life as an errand-boy and will end it as a bookmaker, has pushed himself into a fashionable practice, and a house in Elysium Square?"

"I begin to think," replied Kalogathus, who was becoming restlessly anxious to leave Dumdum, and who was really very unwell, "that I had better make an appointment to see Sir Oxymel Stubbs."

This exalted gentleman, whose very name

almost frightened poor Glybbe into a fit, was not only the President of the Paradoxian College of Physicians, but had taken a leading part in the curing or the killing of many of the princes and statesmen of both hemispheres. The medical baronet's great skill lay in his exact knowledge of the limitations of his calling. His patients went to him, not for what he did, but for what he abstained from doing. He had, however, his foibles as well as his fortes, and one of the former was, to put it in scientific language, a rather grotesque subjectivity. When he himself felt in perfect health there was nothing much the matter with any of those whose tongues he looked at or whose chests he stethoscoped. When he was depressed with any troubles, physical or spiritual (for Sir Oxymel was not less great as a theologian than as a physician), no syllable of hygienic comfort could be extracted from him. Fond of convivial

society in his earlier days, he compensated
any dietetic liberties with himself in the
past by prescribing a relentless austerity
of regimen for those who consulted him
in the present. His formulas were few,
but pithy, and, as Kalogathus was soon by
experience to find out, were repeated with
mechanical precision to all who asked his
advice.

"You have offended," were the first words
of this authority, addressed to his visitor in
the manner of the homilist rather than the
doctor, "against the laws which make for
physical righteousness. At your time of
life you ought to know that Nature never
forgets and never forgives. The idea of
your completing your nervous exhaustion
by scribbling for the *Evening Oracle!*
Nature and Time may or may not do
something for you. Live regularly, occupy
your mind pleasantly, clothe loosely, towel
briskly after your bath, and trust in

Providence. No prescription in the world will do you any good."

And as he said this the great Sir Oxymel Stubbs made a movement which, to Kalogathus, appeared to imply the payment of his fee. The patient deferentially placed a neat paper parcel in the great man's hand, and rejoined Glybbe. Kalogathus intimated his dissent from his friend's optimistic view of the Dumdum faculty, saying rather bitterly, "Surely Sir Oxymel might have done something for me," only to elicit this reproach from his companion :—

"My dear Kalogathus, you are unreasonable. I told you that the Dumdum doctors were the best in the world, and so beyond all doubt they are. Is it possible you should be ignorant that the greatest physicians are those who try to do the least for the sick? The medical men of Dumdum are admitted to be the most scientific in this planet. 'Prognosis,' 'diagnosis,' 'epignosis,' 'metag-

F

nosis,' all these we have, and have carried to great perfection; but 'treatment'! my dear sir, you are sadly behind your time, or you would have known that treatment is an anachronism," and here the citizen of the most practical capital in the world gave a highly superior shrug of his shoulders. "As a sensible man you must see the wisdom of this; nothing could be simpler. If," he jauntily added, "you get well, why then nature has done its work, and if you don't get well all the physicians in the universe could not have made you so."

"In my country," observed Kalogathus, "we should call this sort of thing 'fatalism.'"

"My dear Kalogathus," again interrupted Glybbe, "how often am I to remind you that we Paradoxians are nothing if not practical, and why can't you see the superlative good sense of the Dumdum doctors is shown in hoping nature may do some good when they have found out that they must do harm?"

"In that case," went on the pertinacious visitor, "why have doctors at all?"

"I think," was his host's reply, "you had better put that question to the President of our College of Physicians."

VIII.

The Dumdum hotels being proverbially the cheapest in the most frugal of all capitals, it is needless to say that by this time the visitor from Hilaria found his finances were running low. Dumdum had as many houses and as many inhabitants as ancient Rome.

"The only thing," as Glybbe naïvely admitted, "is that one can never find in Dumdum a residence to suit one; however, to-morrow we will go house-hunting, and try our luck."

On this quest accordingly they went. Mansions capable of housing a legion and a half were forthcoming in plenty. The novel sort of tenements which in the city of the Cæsars were called "insulæ," and which to-day are known as "flats," could be had at a day's notice. These were abodes of enormous altitude, execrably hideous proportions, constructed with a total disregard for the admission of light and the preservation of health. The sleeping-rooms were prison cells without bars to the windows. The domestic offices and servants' dormitories were quite as comfortable sleeping-chambers as cisterns could possibly be made, and their atmosphere was not more injurious to health than cess-pools.

When Kalogathus demurred to all these domiciles in turn, his friend rather irritably said, "Really, if you are so difficult to please, you had better build a house for yourself. You can easily let it again for twice what it costs you."

Kalogathus had now decided upon considerably protracting his stay among the Paradoxians, and sending for his family to join him. He had observed a vacant ground plot in a convenient situation.

"The only difficulty I see about it," was the observation of Glybbe, after hearing of his purpose, "is the question of title."

The legal arrangements and the registry system of Paradoxia were the envy of all neighbouring countries. When, therefore, with a view of negotiating his territorial purchase, Kalogathus called on the man of affairs representing the owners of the property, he was not at all surprised to hear that the combined legal acumen of Dumdum had failed, after years of investigation, to identify the individuals to whom the ground rightly belonged.

"I rather think," with a vague air of hopefulness, remarked our friend's legal adviser, "we have now discovered the man we want; but I am bound to tell you, my good sir," he went on, "there is this risk. By the time your contractor had finished your house the ownership might be disputed; an ejectment suit might be begun, might go against you, and you and your family might be turned out of doors, which," he sympathetically added, "would be very inconvenient, at least for a stranger. The fact is, we in Paradoxia shall not have put these arrangements on a proper footing till we have codified our legal system; and, as you probably know, Dumdum lawyers are too practical to care for anything of this kind. There is only one man in the kingdom who realizes our inconveniences or tries to remedy them, and he is allowed to do nothing, because he is a theorist and a doctrinaire."

"Is there any reason to distrust this reformer?" asked Kalogathus.

"On the contrary," replied the man of business, "there is not the slightest doubt, if he had his way, his plan would end all these confusions and delays at once; but the Dumdum lawyers are, as I tell you, very practical men, and they shrink from a doctrinaire as they would shun the plague."

After a few more interviews, it became plain to Kalogathus that the actual settlement of the doubt which now checked his architectural operations could not reasonably be expected within much less, at the present rate of progress, than half a century. "Truly," he wrote about this time, in a letter to a friend in his own country, "these Paradoxians are the most unaccountable people under the sun. Their idea of legislating is for one of their chambers to undo in a week whatever the other accomplishes in a year. Their system of doctoring is for their great physicians to proclaim their impotence without a blush, and when any one of their number attempts to do anything, to tar and feather him as a 'quack.' Their great lawyers sit in their chambers, pocket their fees, smile at the suits which drag on through decades, and when some jurisconsult shows them how thousands of pounds and scores of years may be saved, he is denounced as a traitor to his cloth, while the great journals of Dumdum hold him up to ridicule as a doctrinaire. I really think," the letter concluded, "it is time for me to be going home."

"Before you leave us," remarked his host, "you must take a run with me across the channel to Blarnia, for your friends will certainly look to you for some information on the great Blarnian question when you are back among them."

The mention of this dependency of Paradoxia recalled to the mind of our traveller some lines in a Paradoxian poet read many years ago, to this effect :—

> "But after being fired at once or twice,
>   The ear becomes more Blarnian, and less nice."

Thus warned, Kalogathus, before acceding to his friend's suggestion, resolved to insure his life, and to make another incursion into the best intellectual circles of Dumdum. Beyond the poet in the scarlet small clothes, he had as yet seen none of the *élite* among the Paradoxian *literati* or *literatuli*.

"To-morrow," was Glybbe's ready promise, "you shall meet as many of these people as you desire, and to begin with, our two chief historians, Cynical Suave and the great Smelfungus, who think so differently on all subjects, that an explosion would follow if they were to be alone together for many minutes."

Suave's writings were well known to our explorer. No one had ever seemed to him so perfectly to handle the Paradoxian language, and to educe such a living melody from its not very musical syllables; for no master of the violin ever obtained more miraculous symphonies from his instrument, or with greater ease, than did Cynical Suave from the tongue that answered with absolute obedience to the lightest touch of his magic pen. The two great men were at this moment within a few feet of each other in the duchess's drawing-room, and as yet there were no signs of a disturbance usually consequent upon the vicinity of acid to alkali. Mr. Suave was an elderly man of upright figure, with a commanding brow, a flute-like voice, in which, with a curiously caressing manner, he continued to say the most disagreeable things impartially about everybody. The compliments which the enthusiastic Kalogathus paid him were overheard by the industrial but irascible Smelfungus. Waiting his opportunity, he beckoned our friend aside into a small divan leading out of the drawing-room itself, and declared himself after this fashion :—

" H'm, h'm," said Smelfungus in his most superior way, "you really speak, my good sir, as if your idea of history was a portrait gallery."

" Not a bad idea, either," the visitor was about blithely to remark, when this austere student of parchment, charters, and muniment-rooms continued :—

" Now in these days history is, above all, a science. What you ought to wish to know is not how men and women formerly lived and loved, dressed and went about, but what the archives, at present being accessible to us, tell you of the great impersonal or ethnological movements of the past."

"That, my good sir," rejoined Kalogathus, "with all due deference to you, is what I care nothing about."

"I suppose, then," rejoined Smelfungus, visibly nettled, "you think that history ought to deal with human beings."

Observing a look of surprise pass over our friend's countenance, this great man continued :—

"That is a very childish view of the historian's business, and it is astounding that an intelligent person, as you seem to be, should cling to so puerile a superstition."

The professor then went on, with peremptory communicativeness, to insist that no really good history of any state or nationality could be written from which human nature was not entirely, or as far as practicable, eliminated.

"Mr. Suave gives you pretty pen-and-ink pictures, and tells you what the people he writes about were really doing and saying; but seriously, do you suppose, my good sir, that sort of thing is history?"

After having apologetically confessed that he did, Smelfungus hissed out :—

"History! It is gossip! You might as well call a society journal," and here, with visible loathing, he pointed to one of these prints on the drawing-room table, "a newspaper. Ask Mr. Dryasdust yonder, the editor of our famous *Antediluvian* periodical whether I am not right, and whether he would publish the personalities which you seem to have mistaken for historical writing."

The conductor of this fossilized organ of Paradoxian criticism being within earshot of the remark, was at once free to confess his unqualified agreement with his friend, the illustrious Smelfungus.

"History," he continued, "should be only the elucidation of impersonal forces, the evolution of formulæ, and these were, of

course, as rigidly impersonal as the Gulf
Stream or the law of gravitation."

For himself he rejoiced to think the
Antediluvian under his control had so
successfully excluded all approach to personality as never to have published a single
article with an ounce of human interest.
The consequence was, and with pride he
confessed it, that the circulation of the
Antediluvian, which under the control of
his predecessor, Joe Babbletongue, was, he
blushed to say, enormous, had now sunk to
zero, and the periodical itself, rather than
pander to the debased taste for personality,
would in six months' time be carried on at
a loss.

After this naïve confession Kalogathus
was scarcely surprised when a few days
later he read in an evening newspaper that
the proprietors of the *Antediluvian*, not
sharing their editor's superiority to the
popular taste, were about to dispense with

Mr. Dryasdust's services, and would probably transfer the control of their periodical
to Mr. Cynical Suave.

"Next week you shall see," was Glybbe's
promise that night to our friend, "some very
illustrious personages, the supreme heads of
our State, at work. A marble monument
is to be unveiled to the great toothpick
reformer of our times; no end of Crimson
Tippets and representatives of sovereignty
itself will be there."

It was a lovely morning, and a picturesque scene. Sculpture was not the forte
of the Paradoxian artists; but the present
was an exception, and the marble effigy of
the late Asclepius Molar about to be, in
the approved Paradoxian phrase, "inaugu-
rated," was unanimously voted a "speaking
likeness" of that defunct benefactor of
humanity.

The carriage and pair containing the
august personage who was to grace the

occasion drove up through a lane of ob-
sequious worshippers—small boys prostrated
themselves before the high-bred steeds,
ladies fluttered perfumed handkerchiefs, and
robust washerwomen, carrying home the
clothes, stopped to see what they could of
the sight, and were so overpowered by the
agitated loyalty of the moment and the
suffocating pressure of the crowd, as only
to keep themselves from fainting by recourse
to a black bottle from the cavernous recesses of their pockets. Illustrated narra-
tives of the life of the exalted being about
to perform the opening ceremony were on
sale, and while they were waiting Kalogathus was able to master the contents of
one of these volumes. Nothing could be
more various than the presentations of the
subject of the little work, or to poor Kalogathus more perplexing. On one page this
sublime being was depicted in the costume
of a field-marshal reviewing his battalions

in the foreground. A little later on the same original had donned the uniform of the Lord High Admiral, glancing complacently from the quarter-deck at the manœuvres of rival squadrons. In another the illustrious creature blazed forth in the crimson and ermine proper to the president of the whole legal system of Paradoxia. Turning over a few more pages, the bewildered Kalogathus descried the same facial lineaments surmounted with the busby of a Muscovite Cossack. The opening illustration of the next chapter in this treatise was that depicting still the same individual disguised as a doctor of theology in the scarlet gown indicating the graduate of Cuckoo Town University. The next surprise of this kaleidoscopic series was the august being habited in the rough tweed and leather gaiters of the Paradoxian sportsman. Yet again he was displayed in the full-dress garb of a member of the

G

Crimson Tippets. After this as a geologist with his hammer; and next, in quick succession, as a yachtsman sweeping the horizon with his spy-glass. Presently the distinguished original presented in this protean fashion was visible in his full length, to the expectant eye of Kalogathus, the wearer of the ordinary frock coat affected by well-to-do Dumdumites, with a well-set-up figure, a cheerful expression, and an indescribable charm of manner.

"Tell me," asked Kalogathus of his companion, "what makes that gentleman so supreme a personage among you? Has he absolute power over the administration of your laws, the sailing of your ships, the mobilization of your troops, the discipline of your universities, or the expenditure of your public moneys?"

"On the contrary," replied Glybbe, evidently taken aback a little at the inquiry, "he is no more above the law than the meanest Paradoxian peasant; as for our church, he only shares its ministrations in common with the poorest in the land; he has no official connection with our fleets; he could not order a single soldier in a line regiment to move an inch; and every fraction of his income is voted for him by the Assembly of the Silent."

"I shall be glad then to know," pursued the indefatigable stranger, "what makes him the first personage in your realm."

"Because," somewhat abruptly replied Glybbe, "he is the representative of a great principle. But I must really tell you, my friend, your inquisitiveness is getting unreasonable; you must be careful, or you will develop into a first-class bore."

IX.

On their journey to the neighbouring coasts of Blarnia, Kalogathus elicited from Glybbe and his fellow-passengers a concise and tolerably consecutive account of the history of that country. Probably no two communities in the world had ever held anything like the relations, long existing between Paradoxia and her dependency, without a decisive rupture. Every incident in their relations was an anomaly, every attempt at reform a paradox, every passing spasm of revolutionary outbreak an absurdity. To begin with, Blarnia had been the gift of a foreign potentate who had no right to dispose of her to a Paradoxian monarch who never desired her possession. The most practical people in the world administered Blarnia on principles diametrically opposed to those underlying the govern-

ment of every other people flying the
Paradoxian flag. The Blarnians had ever
protested that they knew what they wanted
for themselves, and if only they were
allowed to have it, would be loyalty itself
towards the Paradoxian crown. As it was,
their normal condition remained one of
ingrained insurrection and chronic irrecon-
cilability towards their more powerful
neighbour.

"I suppose, then," ventured Kalogathus,
"these Blarnians must be a particularly
cross-grained, ill-conditioned race."

"On the contrary," replied his friend,
"they are, out of Blarnia, the most orderly,
peaceful, and amiable folk imaginable, and
perhaps they might be the same in Blarnia
itself if we only gave them a chance; but
to do this we should have to stoop to see
things with Blarnian eyes, not to ignore
the ethnic peculiarities of the country and
the historic genius of the race. Now it is

a first principle of Paradoxian statesmanship that an imperial people such as we Paradoxians are cannot, with any regard for our own dignity, demean ourselves to do this. Just as Smelfungus writes his history on abstract principles, so we insist upon ruling Blarnia upon our own *a priori* ideas. The day of Paradoxian greatness would be gone, and our imperial glory departed for ever, when we condescended to do otherwise."

Glybbe was in ordinary matters a cool-headed and unemotional person; he waxed excited in manner and flushed in face while he enunciated these sentiments. It struck Kalogathus that he had read words to exactly the same effect in a morning newspaper, from which he suspected Glybbe to derive his ideas on every subject, for the business of journalism in Paradoxia is not so much to guide public opinion as to intensify private prejudice.

After many years of anarchy and blood-shed, certain Paradoxian statesmen were now endeavouring to remedy the real evils of Blarnia, and to supply her true wants. The attempt was proving slowly successful, but Kalogathus was fully prepared to find the Paradoxian administrators, for persevering in this attempt, denounced as revolutionary fanatics and derided as bookish doctrinaires. It was not easy, as Kalogathus found after a few days in Blarnia, to elicit a candid opinion from the natives of their grievances and wants.

"You seem," he said to a peasant at a fair, "to be very prosperous here just now."

"Your honour may well say that," was the cheerful reply.

"And yet," observed the visitor, "I see signs of sad poverty in some places."

"True to you, your honour," at once responded the same speaker; "it's clane dying for want we are from one year's end to another."

"And yet you have all probably got a tidy little sum in the savings bank."

"Bedad!" observed this complaisant patriot, "we could just pave all the way from Fair Head to Waterford Harbour with golden guineas."

Having made several further attempts in his usual truth-seeking spirit to reach the real facts of the case, and having in every instance received replies in comparison with which the answers of the Sphinx would be lucidity itself, Kalogathus desisted at last from interrogation, but, keeping his eyes wide open, concluded that the true condition of Blarnia was neither worse nor better than that of most other countries on this imperfect planet.

While Kalogathus and his friends were seated over their dessert in one of the chief hotels of a thriving Blarnian town, Glybbe, who prided himself upon being all things to all men, carelessly took up a pair of nut-crackers, and handling them in such a manner as to suggest the image of a pistol, said, with something like a wink to the Blarnian gentleman sitting opposite to him—

"Had much of this sort of thing lately?"

"Ah! and if you only knew more about us, you might have known the divil a bit of shooting have we in Old Blarnia to brighten us up now."

The words had scarcely left the speaker's mouth when a crashing sound was heard beneath his feet, and a small bullet, very unceremoniously making its entrance through the floor, shattered the speaker's plate, and knocked out of his fingers the filbert he was about to place in his mouth. A shock-headed waiter, rushing into the room, said—

" Beg pardon, gentlemen, but thought you

would wish to know they only fired in the air."

It turned out that in this particular town, where shooting was so utterly unknown, a duelling party had been improvised for the special amusement of Kalogathus in the apartment immediately beneath. The two principals, who were of mixed Blarno-Columbian descent, and both furnished with patent Columbian "hair-triggers," had determined to settle their differences by the ordeal of battle across the dinner-table, with this result. The excitement soon proved contagious, and the single pistol-shot had awoke the most pugnacious echoes of the whole place. In half an hour a free faction-fight worthy of the best days of Adelphi melodrama was raging merrily outside. The fact proved to be that the great Paradoxian statesman, bent upon descending to posterity as the pacificator of Blarnia, had unexpectedly arrived. He was given,

of course, a really Blarnian welcome.
The next morning Kalogathus, from his
dressing-room window, looked down upon
a scene of charred timbers and ruined
walls.

On his return to Dumdum a few days
later, our visitor was dining at the house
of one of the astutest members of that semi-
foreign army of occupation who control
much of the commerce of Paradoxia, the
Count Vieuxchateau. This gentleman was
not socially very agreeable, but his opportunities of knowledge were large, his
criticism was impartial, his opinion was
worth having. Commenting on our friend's
surprise, provoked by the condition of
Blarnia, at the haphazard manner in which
the imperial affairs of Dumdum were conducted, the count expressed himself as
follows :—

"If the business of my firm were man-
aged with as little method as the affairs of

the Paradoxian Empire are administered, I
should in a fortnight's time not have a
capable clerk in my employ, and after six
months my house, which has survived the
wreck of dynasties and the crash of empires, would be hopelessly insolvent. Come
and lunch with me any day in Obolus Alley
at three o'clock, you will find us all there,
and you may perhaps learn a thing or
two."

This was the greatest compliment paid
Kalogathus during his sojourn in Dumdum.
Only men whom Count Vieuxchateau
deemed of real consequence were ever
invited to the hospitalities of Obolus
Alley.

The truth is, the contributions of our
friend to the Paradoxian press, and especially
to the select periodical whose editor boasted
that he drew the line at barons, had won
him a considerable reputation in the land of
his stay. Had he been able to prolong his

sojourn, he would certainly, together with the accomplished Simian, now everywhere famous as Monsieur FitzDaisy, have been invited to visit in royal state the first magistrate at the most famous castle in the Paradoxian kingdom, but the hospitalities paid to the two were drawing to a close. Monsieur FitzDaisy pined for the society of his kind in the Ethiopian jungle; Kalogathus himself desired to return to his modest property in his native Hilaria.

The only invitation which the two had accepted and which as yet remained unfulfilled was to a *fête champêtre* at the Porphyry Hall, a stately palace with magnificent grounds famed for its pyrotechnical displays, in the suburbs of Dumdum. The two drove down together in Monsieur Fitz-Daisy's victoria. All the rank and fashion of the Paradoxian metropolis were there. Before dinner, illuminated addresses were presented, with silver caskets to enclose them, to "the two most illustrious guests of the year, Signor Kalogathus and Monsieur FitzDaisy, on the eve of their return to their native countries."

The heart of the generous ape was really touched while he read the parchment; he was pricked by the thought of his perhaps too severe criticisms on Paradoxian man-hood, womanhood, and humanity generally. He averted his head, lifted up a highly-laced pocket-handkerchief to his eyes, for, like the sensitive and high-bred brute that he was, he could not repress a tear at this fresh display of kindness on the part of the human relatives whom so discourteously he had repudiated.

The firework display, the closing scene of the gala programme, was about to terminate. The artist had expended his supreme efforts in the set piece, now awaited with breathless excitement.

After a blaze of " Roman candles," a coruscation of "rockets," and a sustained brilliancy of " Sicilian lights," there were discerned from the terrace on which the spectators were, two dazzling and multi-coloured presentments of the guests of the evening.

Monsieur FitzDaisy and Signor Kalogathus shook each other's hands with convulsive warmth as they beheld the effigies of their two selves vividly traced in resplendent hues thrown out into magnificent relief against a dark background, scientifically arranged to heighten the display and intensify the effect.

Arm in arm, the two friends, the observant man and the hypercritical ape, descended the stairs, entered the victoria, drove back to Dumdum, and the next day started for their respective homes. But the final spectacle they had beheld long dwelt before their mental vision, and the

applausive thunders which bade them fare-
well in the palace of the Porphyry Hall
can even to this day be recalled by their
appreciative ears.

How the "House of Lords Question" was Settled

A TALE OF THE TERRACE

OR, MRS. PONSONBY-JONES'S REVENGE

I.

A HOUSE OF COMMONS LADY HER FRIENDS AND FOES

THIS is the way in which it all came about. Even that most indefatigable squire of dames, Mr. Hazelrig, Leader of the Popular Chamber in Lord Fitztempest's Government in the early days of the twentieth century, was beginning to think that the House of Commons Terrace looking over the Thames might do with a little of the favour shown it during the

H 97

season by Mrs. Ponsonby-Jones and her vivacious sisters. This lady, the wife of a prosperous north-country member, exulted over some remains of youth and beauty. She possessed, indeed, married daughters and grandchildren. But her complexion often reproduced the freshness of her teens; and if juvenile manners and still more juvenile dress can redeem matronhood from age, Mrs. Ponsonby-Jones was not more than five-and-twenty. She had been one of the first Parliamentary ladies to discover the opportunities, social and amatory, of the Terrace. She and her daughters, it was calculated, had eaten more strawberries and drunk more cups of tea on that agreeable elevation than all the other Parliamentary womankind of the United Kingdom put together. The whips could not get their men to sit out debates, or failed at the critical moment to marshal them into the division lobby. The explanation was that honourable gentlemen were ministering to the wants of the fair invaders of St. Stephen's, headed by their dauntless captain in petticoats. Other members' womankind were encouraged by such an example. The counter attractions of the Terrace withdrew an increasing number of the younger M. P.'s from their duties to their constituents within the House itself. The newspapers took up the subject. Articles going near to breach of privilege impiously compared the riparian purlieus of the Chamber to the old Cremorne or to the more recent Empire Theatre. Questions, transparently pointed at Mrs. Ponsonby-Jones and her "monstrous regiment," were asked of the First Commissioner of Works and the Home Secretary. Petitions on the subject began to pour in. The "first representative assembly in the world" was manifestly being brought into contempt. Public opinion proclaimed that something must be done.

II.

THE HOUSE OF COMMONS AND MRS. PONSONBY-JONES'S INVASION

At last the head of the Government, Lord Fitztempest, conferred seriously with his second in command, the Chancellor of the Exchequer, Mr. Hazelrig, as to how the scandal should be dealt with. The Premier had a very low opinion of the Popular House ever since he himself ceased to sit in it. He disliked it at this moment more than ever, because Mrs. Ponsonby-Jones was his personal detestation. Lady Fitztempest had lately taken up the she-parliamentarian with the double-barrelled name, who was therefore a great deal too much at Stormont House, to the Premier's unconcealed disgust.

III.

THE PRIME MINISTER'S THUNDER-BOLT

Presently it became known that Lord Fitztempest was resolved to deal with the abuse by a *coup d'état*.   Three Cabinets were held within a week.   As the result of these, Mr. Hazelrig brought forward a proposal curtly declaring that the presence of lady guests within the precincts of Parliament was not in the interests of public business.   Mrs. Ponsonby - Jones had her men ready to oppose the motion.   Her husband, a meek little person, who never presumed to appear in the same drawing-room as his wife, made his maiden speech against it.   But the House was in one of its hot fits.   There was an all-night sitting. The lady - killers and philanderers of the

Assembly carried obstruction to unprecedented lengths. But at 3 a.m. on the morning of August 11th the Ministerial proposal was carried by a three to one majority. The House of Commons had seen the last for some time of Mrs. Ponsonby-Jones.

IV.

MRS. PONSONBY-JONES'S REVENGE

The real Parliamentary struggle with the lady of a north-country member was, however, only beginning. That indefatigable amazon congratulated herself that her duel with the peer-Premier had been delayed until the suppressed sex had ceased to exist, and women throughout the United Kingdom shared with men a vote in returning members to Westminster.

The organization which got rid of Free Trade was insignificant by the side of that which Mrs. Ponsonby-Jones and her friends prepared for getting rid of the House of Lords. No such display of stateswomanship had ever been witnessed or dreamed of. That which democratic dukes and communistic earls had in vain threatened against an assembly wherein a perverse destiny had afflicted them with seats, was soon in a fair way of being accomplished by this amazing champion of the rejected *habituées* of the Ladies' Terrace. With her favourite cavalier, the Cambridge revolutionary, Mr. Dynamite Lamb, Mrs. Ponsonby-Jones visited every town of importance in the United Kingdom. Richly secured against all material want for the coming winter was any household whose head had agreed to vote for the anti-peer candidate. The consequence of these tactics was the return to St. Stephen's of that memorable majority pledged to the cry of "Down with the Lords!" When

Mr. Dynamite Lamb carried in the House of Commons his carefully-balanced resolution, providing that the hereditary body should, as at present constituted, cease under existing conditions to form part of the legislature, Lord Fitztempest took the matter with a coolness that surprised everybody. Mr. Hazelrig had already, in the Commons, created a sensation by provisionally accepting Mr. Lamb's scheme, subject only to the definition of the circumstances which were to regulate the supersession of the peers.

Here the matter remained for some time. Meanwhile, the lady voters having proved their power in the constituencies by enabling Mrs. Ponsonby-Jones to whip up a majority for Mr. Lamb, the more aggressively ambitious spirits of the sex decided that their demonstrated ability to control the legislature entitled them to a Chamber of their own. This suggestion met with as little resistance from Mr. Hazelrig on behalf of the Government as had been encountered by the preceding reform. The reason was that Lord Fitztempest, after secret and searching inquiry throughout the kingdom, had satisfied himself of the possibility, greatly to his own party's advantage, of a compromise between the peers and their erstwhile antagonist, Mrs. Ponsonby-Jones.

v.

THE FITZTEMPEST-PONSONBY-JONES COMPROMISE

This solution turned out, in fact, to be an offer from the Premier to the victorious lady to divide the spoils of conquest between them in a fashion that should be satisfactory to the honour of each. Lord Fitztempest had been described graphically, and more or less correctly, by an appreciative critic as a mass of putty painted to look like granite. He was also a political pessimist of a constitutionally cynical turn. That things were doomed to go hopelessly wrong in this democratic day was his conviction. That one surrender or blunder more or less made very little difference was his unfailing solace. No person had yet proposed to deprive the peers of their titles, their estates, or social precedence. Under these circumstances their lordships displayed an alacrity, which Mrs. Ponsonby-Jones had not anticipated, to agree with their assailants while yet there was time, and by a seasonable reform to obviate their constitutional extinction.

The idea was to assimilate the operations of the Hereditary Chamber to those of the Privy Council, which never meets save when it is specially summoned. In other words, Lord Fitztempest and Mr. Hazelrig between them brought in a Bill relieving their lordships of habitual attendance on the crimson benches, and enacting that henceforward they should only use the painted Chamber when required by the Sovereign to revise, particularly in the department of foreign policy, the discussions and decisions of the elective legislature.

Meanwhile, as it was a self - evident anomaly that the ladies of England should be trusted with a parliamentary franchise, and yet prevented from actually forming a part of the legislature, the citizenesses of the country should henceforth return deputies of their own to Westminster, who could transact their affairs on the premises of the peers on such occasions as their lordships were without any summons to Westminster.

The speech in which Lord Fitztempest supported this proposal was quite humorous and almost convincing. Many years ago, he reminded their lordships, one of their own number had objected to the admission of peeresses to the gallery as spectators of their debate on the ground that it would make the House look like a casino. Now, Lord Fitztempest suggested, his brother peers ought to be thankful that they had saved something of the earlier privileges of their order and their sex, that the Chamber was not to be unconditionally surrendered to its fair besiegers, and that those who had been its sole owners would yet have a place to meet in when they were wanted, which, he characteristically added, would not be very often.

It had long been a maxim with the political press on the Premier's side to applaud the anticipation of your enemy's innovations whenever you had the chance, on the plea that it was better to be robbed or reformed by a friend than by an enemy. This was the principle on which Lord Fitztempest and his friends had, years ago, given the country gratuitous and compulsory education, and had trumped the Radical card of manhood suffrage by the Tory card of male and female adult franchise, with the eventual consequences in the year 19— which have been set forth faithfully in this historic narrative.

How I became Prime Minister

BY AN UP-TO-DATE POLITICIAN

IT had been a family idea from nursery days. When, therefore, other lads were wasting their time over their games I was showing those about me that I had what is called a "personality" which was all my own, or was learning in its different aspects the art of advertisement.

"This boy," said the examiner who came to our grammar school, as he looked over my essay, "will surely come to the Cabinet if he does not stop at the gallows."

When, therefore, it was known that I was going to stand for a scholarship at the university, my reputation had preceded me thither. Before they met in the college

chapel to elect, the dons had all agreed
that I was to be the man. I had not
tried to be brilliant or deep. In Latin and
Greek, above all in the "Taste" paper, I
might have been beaten by much less
successful youths ; but before the examination was half over the quaint and unexpected things written by James Jerkin
(the English for the old French house of
de Jerquand) had been repeated with
sniggers in half the common - rooms of
the place. The same luck followed me
when I went into residence. Apart from
luck with books and examinations, before
my first term was over Jerkin of John's was
as well known as the proctor's bulldog. In
societies where I felt sure of my ground I
spread amazement, when I was in the vein,
by uttering sentiments remembered to this
day. I was far too wise to fritter my
talents away only on the studies of the
place. I took indeed a first-class in my

Little-go examination, and followed it up with two other first-classes afterwards. But I worked at my cricket a good deal harder. I made myself, with more labour than my studies ever cost me, the first batsman in the place, and the second best wicket-keeper in England. In those days the newspapers were just glanced at alike by undergraduates and dons; they were never really read. I rightly judged, therefore, that one who could possess himself of the cream of the daily prints would startle those about him more than if he made all Aristotle and Plato his own. Of course, though it was not then exactly the "swagger thing" to do, I went in for speaking at the Union. Not as a regular thing, but reserving myself for great occasions. First, having made them promise not to repeat it to a soul, I told one, and then another, that I might perhaps say a few words that night on the motion for or against the Government, which was to be brought forward by the champion speaker among the boys.

By the time that I got back to college for lunch, the news that Jerkin of John's was to speak that night was all over the place. "Surprisingly mature views for a mere youth!" "Extraordinary aptness of illustration!" these were the comments on the eloquence which was the distilled essence of that newspaper reading which superior spirits affected to despise. Soon after this men and dons, gathering together in the college gardens after breakfast, said with bated breath to each other: "Have you heard? Jerkin speaks to-night!"

Encouraged by this reception, I resolved to show them that, if I had not before carried off university prizes, it was not from lack of power to do so. I sported my oak against all comers, kept a tea-kettle perpetually boiling on my hob, cooled my head with relays of wet towels, omitted

I

no other precautions to ensure success, and swept the board of academic prizes, but never relaxed my cricket or other athletic prowess. For one person who reads a three-line paragraph of university intelligence, there are at least a dozen who read a cricket score at Lord's.

The sequel showed how right I was. In due course I ate my dinners and was called to the Bar. No solicitor knew, or cared to know, if I was that Jerkin of John's who was the only treble first-class of his year. But every lawyer, when he heard my name, and his clerk brought me my brief, wished to make sure that I was none other than the Jerkin who in one season had made five "centuries" and not out, and stumped three men in one over.

The same record that had helped me so much at the Bar carried everything before it in the constituency. The first time of standing I was returned at the head of the poll. That place I never lost. To treat real work as play, to go in for play in a spirit of deadly earnest, this is not a bad rule for success in life. It is a sure way for coming to the front in politics, whether at Westminster or in the provinces. My own party was in opposition. My leader hinted to me that the hour had come when a question framed in a certain way which he suggested, and containing damaging innuendoes, might put the Government in a tight place. The question was asked. Before all its effects were over it did more than that; it put Ministers on the left side of the Speaker, for it supplied a pretext for a censure-resolution, which my authorship of the question that had led up to it entitled me to move. Of course, it was understood that I should have a place in the incoming Administration.

My old friends, the newspapers, once

more did me a good turn; the memory
of my university prestige did me a better.
The burden of press, of lobbies, and of
smoking-rooms was that James Jerkin had
long been the coming man, that no person
represented national opinion so faithfully as
he, and that the new Premier would do
well to take him into the Cabinet. Into
the Cabinet, therefore, without stopping at
any intermediate office, I came at a bound.
Some people hinted a few spiteful things.
One editor, of whose name I made a note,
applied to me the pointless platitude about
the ascent of the rocket and the descent
of the stick. By this time, as may be
supposed, I had become something of a
personage among the people as well as
in Parliament. Some mischievous toadies
there were who, thinking, I suppose, to
please me, put in paragraphs about the
antiquity of my Anglo-Norman ancestors,
the de Jerquands of Angoulême. Now,

nothing irritates the average member of the English democracy so much as for it to be hinted that his neighbour is his better by birth. Quick as thought, therefore, and publicly as the sun itself, I disclaimed the patrician impeachment. In one of my speeches to my constituents I plainly said, that though the de Jerquands might have worn chain-armour during the Second Crusade, and might be a very famous stock, I knew and wished to know nothing of them.

"No, ladies and gentlemen!" I went on, "it is a poor name, but it is my own. James Jerkin, son of Jeremiah of that ilk, Anglo-Saxon on both sides, a plain person, but a loyal son of the people."

That deliverance was received with cheers which might have been heard from the North Foreland to Beachy Head. A friendly pencil in next week's *Punch* depicted James Jerkin in an assembly of his countrymen declining a Frenchified baron's coronet which had been offered him. "Our Jimmy," or "The People's Jerkin," were the titles with which I was next greeted, which have never deserted me, and which I have, I hope, done nothing to disgrace.

In the part of the country that I represented at St. Stephen's the humble ass was the quadruped most extensively employed for purposes of locomotion. The complaint locally prevailed that the breed of donkeys was not what it used to be. Clearly, therefore, it was the first duty of a patriot to stop this degeneration. To breed shorthorns, to nurse orchids under glass roofs, might do for other statesmen. To me there remained the less decorative, but more useful, part of improving the stock and elevating the lot of the lowliest, though not the least faithful, of the four-footed friends of man. From the streets of Cairo to the heights of Hampstead, from the

banks of the Nile to the beacons of
Malvern, such an enterprise must secure
applause. A philanthropic peer, now de-
ceased, had scarcely heard of my plan
before he hailed me on the platform as
just the friend which humanity wanted.
The costermongers of Whitechapel took
their cue from him, hymned me in songs
which made my name a household word
in the East End. A little later, as good
luck would have it, the favourite donkey
that drew a Royal lady's chair went to its
rest. I made interest enough in high places
to be allowed to fill the vacancy with the
sweetest little Neddy you ever saw in your
life from my Midland breeding farm. The
gift and its reception went straight to the
popular heart, like the rifle-ball of the
winner of the Queen's Prize to the bull's-
eye at Bisley.

Successes like these, of course, made me
enemies. Shallowby Humm, to whose

David from boyhood I had played Jona-
than, said several rather unkind things.
Dyce Digby rudely wanted to know how
long donkeymania and Jerkinmania would
last.

"Long enough," said I to myself, "to
see you both out, my fine gentlemen."

The Right Honourable Timothy Highlow,
now in opposition, but whom in early days
I had helped to office, had to confess that
in the race for public favour my donkeys
had beaten his jampots. It was, in fact,
for some time a duel between the "People's
Tim," as Highlow had been called, and the
"People's Jim," as I was now known. But
with so thoroughly up-to-date a politician
as myself, Tim could not be in it with Jim.

Every great man, someone has said
truly, creates the taste by which he is
enjoyed. Certainly this has been always
true of me. The sanitation of St. Stephen's
is proverbially bad, Strange that before

me it should have occurred to no one
that the inveterate miasma was caused
by the accumulation of decomposed jokes
and stories stale to suffocation. When I
first entered the House it literally reeked
of Latin grammar tags and of mouldy
quotations from Roman poets, whom
M.P.'s found it easier to quote than they
would have done to construe. Before I
had been installed a session on my corner
seat below the gangway I had changed
all this, and let in an atmosphere of
thoughts and allusions which freshened
and sweetened the place. French *opera
bouffe*, instead of Lempriere, supplied my
allusions, quotations, and tropes. The men
about me had forgotten the little Latin
and Greek they ever knew. They did
occasionally run over to Paris to enjoy
the latest fun of the Boulevards; or if
they satisfied themselves instead with the
accounts in a society paper, they would

have been indignant if they had been
found out. Some of my happiest hits
were said by those who heard them to
make them feel as if their time had been
passed at the Café Riche or Anglais instead of at Westminster. As it is the
day of travel made cheap, so do we live
in the hour of knowledge made easy.
High rhetoric on provincial platforms did
very well a hundred years ago for Canning
at Liverpool or Plymouth, for Sir Robert
Peel at Tamworth; but it was not at all
the sort of thing for the " People's Jim."
Odds and ends of useful knowledge,
familiar and forgotten truths in geography,
astronomy, meteorology—anything, in fact,
from Shakespeare to musical glasses—these,
neatly arranged and wisely introduced, made
my provincial speeches a little education to
those who heard them. Some scoffers said
it reminded them of the Polytechnic and
Professor Pepper. But in popular speaking,

as in duelling, the great thing is to fire low. Critics might smile, but I never went over the heads of my audience, and the laugh, I take it, really lay with me.

Meanwhile things were getting into a mess both at Westminster and elsewhere. The "People's Tim" had become a misnomer, for the people would not follow him. Every minute, someone has said, if rightly used, is travel. But though the minutes of his life would have made a pretty large sum, Mr. Highlow had been a good many years without getting "much forrarder." He had reason to regret taking me at his own price rather than at mine before he had done with it. But I was now nearly big enough to set up on my own account. Some trouble with Dyce Digby I had. You see, we had been for long years such close friends that men spoke of us as a "party of two." But Dyce Digby was a creature of impulse, and took his pleasures not wisely but too well.   There are few men, M.P.'s or not M.P.'s, who can give, if closely examined and "shadowed," an account of themselves at every moment during the twenty-four hours which will quite satisfy a jury of old women such as it is easy to strike in the House of Commons.   Private inquiry agents are great blessings to the man who has his way to make, as I had, and is not squeamish about trifles, as it was never my weakness to be.   Wherever Dyce Digby went, on horse or foot, by road or rail, there was he observed by some ubiquitous agent of my friend, Mr. Pollaky.   In less than a year we had got together material against him which would have filled a whole library of scandalous chronicles.   Obviously such a man as this was not fit to retain the confidence of the husbands and fathers in the borough which he represented.   Dyce Digby, therefore, was given a hint to go.   He has never

found a way of getting back to the House of
Commons.   This is what the men of science
call the survival of the fittest, which in this
case happens to be myself.   For one by
nature not unamiable the processes were
scarcely pleasant.   But the command of
patriotism silenced all scruples, and when
the finger of one's country beckons one on,
one can only follow—so at least the world
will read in the autobiography which, like
the rest of them, I shall employ my next
turn of Opposition in writing.   Dyce Digby
safely buried under several cartloads of
scandal in private life, only one serious rival
remained.

Except in some few points of temperament, Rupert Oxford was a natural likeness
of myself.   In some ways more quick to
see the private bearing of any public
question, not less resourceful, Oxford had
a trick of worrying himself about trifles
which to weak nerves means the grave or

the madhouse—in any case failure—and from which I was always free. No fidgety woman was ever "drawn" so easily. Outside Parliament people liked him none the worse for his tantrums, his pets, and sulks. Such a man, I saw, was sure, if wisely baited, to exhaust himself before middle age. Poor Oxford quarrelled with everyone—with the press, with his social toadies, with his leader, with his whole party, last of all with me. That was fatal, as is generally the case to persons who won't make way for the "People's Jim." He had a pretty funeral. Just to show there was no ill-feeling, I followed his body to the grave and went into demi-mourning for three weeks.

I had now been master of the House of Commons for two years, not troubling it with set speeches in the old stately style, but addressing it in committee as one speaks at the directors' board, and on second

readings as at the annual meeting of share-
holders. The plan succeeded even beyond
my hopes. The most powerful newspapers
found that in a business age what Parliament wanted was a business man who had
studied all the American notions, and whose
ideas were thoroughly up to date.

When the "People's Tim" disappeared,
there was a general demand that his place
should be taken by the "People's Jim."
But it was not to be. A Court intrigue
placed Lord Fitzbooby in the post which
should have been mine. Great was the
national disgust. The costermongers from
the East End met in the majesty of their
millions to protest against the slight on
me. All Britons, grateful for my services
to the race of donkeys, joined in these
representations.

During his short premiership, poor Lord
Fitzbooby never went back to his house in
Grosvenor Square without a nervous glance

to see whether his windows had been broken in his absence. Whenever he heard a boy whistling in the street, the tune was sure to be a music - hall song written by the Laureate, bidding him, with all speed, make way for the " People's Jim."

When the next vacancy occurred, every-one knew I could not be passed over again. An East End demonstration was to be held in a West End park, which my residence overlooked. The gates had been closed. The mob was like to pull down the railings. At this moment I showed myself on my balcony.

"Good people," I said, in tones audible throughout the multitude, "pray go peace-fully to your homes. These things are in greater than human hands ; be sure, as I am, that all will be for the best."

Such high-souled, disinterested patriotism struck a chord and roused an enthusiasm for me which carried all hostile cabals before it, and against which no petty intrigues could prevail. I alone, as the press with one voice said, had prevented a riot, perhaps averted a revolution. Dyce Digby, Rupert Oxford, the great Mr. Highlow himself were all now out of the way. Nothing remained for me but to perform a railway journey from a West End terminus to a historic building in a home county, and to go through an interesting ceremony, the details of which nothing would induce me to divulge, but the effect of which was to establish me in my remarkably secure position on the right hand of the Speaker's Chair.

K

How his Party lost Mr. Contango

I.

WHAT LED TO THE INCIDENT

BELGRAVE SQUARE, a fine morning in the height of the season. Lady Dilly, wife of Sir Hector Dilly, the chief parliamentary Whip of his party, turns from the window, out of which she has been looking in silent disgust during the last ten minutes, and says rather petulantly to her husband—

"So those odious people next door are having the red carpet and the awning put out again. I suppose they are entertaining to-night; how very provoking, and my reception evening, too!"

To explain the situation, it need only be said that Mr. Contango, the first City gentleman who had ever settled in Belgrave Square, had recently gratified his own and his wife's social ambitions by buying the lease of an eligible mansion next door to that owned by Sir Hector Dilly, the Whip of the party with which Mr. Contango, when at Westminster, voted. Lady Dilly was now celebrating her first Belgravian season, and had issued cards for a dance on this particular night to the music of the fashionable Red Magyar Band. In themselves, the wives, both of the party official and of the prosperous stockbroker, were pleasant, amiable ladies. Both, however, were rather pretty women. Both had their social aspirations, the one long since in process of realization, the other at last seeming in a fair way of attainment. The two, therefore, seemed to each other to move in orbits dangerously close. Mrs. Contango was the daughter of a pauper baronet of ancient lineage. She knew that Lady Dilly, for all her airs, as she said, had been promoted by her husband from a country vicarage to share the honours of his by no means ancient baronetcy. Lady Dilly being the hostess of her party, and Mrs. Contango the wife of a very wealthy member of it, the two ladies were on visiting terms ; that is, they exchanged calls as seldom as decency allowed. Mrs. Contango, on the strength of her family descent, assumed, perhaps unintentionally, to the Whip's wife a defensive attitude which had much annoyed that stateswoman. Mrs. Contango reflected that she was better born, as her looking-glass told her quite as attractive as, and, as her husband's cheques proclaimed, certainly wealthier than the Whip's lady. Lady Dilly, on the other hand, was admitted universally to be nothing less than perfectly charming. She was a clever woman with intellectual tastes, and in the eyes of the world with faultless tact. But, as the members of her own household knew, she was not a person whose sunlight it was safe to intercept. She had in truth been spoiled by years of worship from those who followed Sir Hector in the St. Stephen's lobbies. Above everything, Lady Dilly was admitted by all whom she considered good judges to be incomparable as a chatelaine and a hostess. Since Mr. Paramount, the Prime Minister, had lost his wife, she had done the chief entertaining for the party, and was allowed to manage her hospitalities with great grace and skill. She lived, as she proudly reflected, in the best house in the most aristocratic square in London, and if inhabitants of Berkeley or Grosvenor Square might have challenged this description, they had never done so to Lady Dilly's knowledge. It seemed, therefore, something like sacrilege when the residence

next to her own in that august enclosure
was appropriated by a gentleman who had
offices in Threadneedle Street.   Nor did
this dissatisfaction become less when Lady
Dilly found that in a quiet way her new
neighbour had an individuality of her own
which she was not prepared to efface even
under the social shadow of the Whip's wife.

Independently of her ladyship's prejudices,
Mrs. Contango developed her programme
for the season with as light a heart and
in as little awe of mightier rivals as if,
instead of being in Belgravia's patrician
centre, she was in Bayswater.   These
thoughts were in Lady Dilly's mind while
she poured out Sir Hector's tea, and found
expression from her pretty lips while the
baronet was munching his toast, and Faudel,
the butler, was constantly entering the room
to lay fresh telegrams or letters by his
master's plate.

II.

WHERE ARE THE RED MAGYARS?

Sir Hector Dilly's head serving-man was always ready to reflect on an exaggerated scale her ladyship's unconcealed disgust at the presumption of, as the Dilly butler called them, "the noovoo reesh" next door. When, an hour or two later, he went, according to his habit, for his noonday draught to the sign of the " Running Foot-man," the chosen haunt of the below-stairs gentlemen, in or out of livery, in the district, he had conceived a sense of personal grievance at the thought of the stock-broker's lady venturing to entertain on the same night on which his mistress was "to receive," to meet Mr. Paramount and a royal duke himself. He scowled viciously

as he eyed from the pavement the prepara-
tions for the evening's entertainment, and
emitted a distinct oath when he was nearly
tripped up by the roll of the but partially
unfolded crimson cloth on which the dainty
feet of the stockbroker's guests were that
night to tread.   Standing with others of his
order at the bar of the " Running Footman,"
the ruffled Faudel overheard a glowing
account from a Contango menial of the
dance whose music was to be played by
the famous Red Magyars.   Faudel said
nothing, but took a resolution the fruits of
which were to be visible a few hours later.

Sir Hector Dilly, a short-tempered man
with an autocratic manner, as is often the
case with party Whips, was visibly ruffled
when he sat down to luncheon in Belgrave
Square that day.

"Could anything be done to stop these
proceedings?" was the question which, with
the sweet unreasonableness of her sex, Lady

Dilly, still fretting at the thought of the Contango entertainment, had asked.

"Well," was the Whip's grim reply, "without buying up the whole square or the foreign bandsmen, I do not see, my dear, how we can interfere."

These words, overheard by Faudel, gave him, as he put it to a friend, a "notion." In the course of his afternoon stroll, he found himself near the headquarters of the Red Magyar instrumentalists. There is some reason for thinking that he himself had business there.

III.

WHAT HAPPENED AT MRS. CONTANGO'S DANCE

Between 10 and 11 p.m. nearly all Mrs. Contango's guests had arrived in Belgrave Square. The last palm tree had long since been placed in its appointed niche; the last

Chinese lantern had been lighted under the balcony awning. Nothing was wanted but the musicians that dancing might begin. At last it was within measurable distance of midnight. Not a human being in the romantic uniform of the Red Magyars was in sight. The guests were looking curiously at each other; poor Mrs. Contango moved about like a lost spirit, and wished that the earth would swallow her up.

Mr. Contango, a gentleman of resource and penetration, saw the trick which had been played on him; resolved to be even yet with his wife's persecutors; and perceived in an instant how, the Red Magyars notwithstanding, the ball might be saved from being an entire fiasco.

In five minutes more he was in a cab whirling towards a famous music-hall. Money was, of course, no consideration to Mr. Contango. He had not, therefore, much difficulty in arranging with the manager for an immediate despatch of a sufficient number of qualified instrumentalists to play as long as his guests could dance. And dance they did with a good will to re-assure Mrs. Contango, whom everyone liked, and everyone pitied on the disappointment which she had received.

IV.

MR. CONTANGO'S REPRISAL

Shortly after this incident Mr. Contango's attendance at the House of Commons became more irregular than ever. His indifference to the edicts of the Whip was most marked. The society papers had, of course, got hold of the ball in Belgrave Square, and had hinted pretty directly that the Red Magyars had failed at the command of a rival hostess. This, as readers of these lines know, was not entirely correct.

Morally, however, there may have been something in what these prints said.

Be that as it may, Mr. Contango, a short, choleric gentleman, with a face and neck suggestive of apoplexy, decided that the moment had come for him, in his own phrase, to break the glasses. He had long been disgusted with the exclusiveness of the leaders of the party which he had incautiously joined, and now bluntly told Sir Hector Dilly and his understrapper that they need send him no more of their underscored whips.

The chief club of the party hostile to that which Sir Hector Dilly served was next door in Pall Mall from their opponents' headquarters. A malcontent with Mr. Contango's means was not likely to be disregarded by tacticians so shrewd as Sir Hector Dilly's rivals. Mr. Contango found, as might have been expected, that he had inadvertently associated in the past with politicians whom he really did not approve, and that his chief, Mr. Paramount, and his minion, Sir Hector Dilly, were between them ruining the country. He had no sooner begun to recant his past errors than the anti-Paramountites received him with open arms, electing him into the great club of their party.

Shortly after this the general election came. How the Paramount majority of 300 was changed into a minority of 152 is a fact of political history. Whether incidents of the Contango ball in Belgrave Square and the private feelings of men like Mr. Contango on these and other matters of socio-political intercourse contributed to that result is, of course, a subject of speculation, but is, there seems reason to believe, by no means improbable.

The New Waitress

I.

WHAT MRS. PHILANDER THOUGHT OF THE HOUSE OF COMMONS

MRS. PHILANDER was the pretty and generally amiable wife of Mr. Theodore Philander, the rising member for the Midland constituency of Hilborough. She was really fond of her husband. She had a restless craving for social position. With the idea of gratifying this ambition she had encouraged her Theodore to enter the House of Commons, on the plea that it could not but help to improve his practice at the Bar. The delusion is a common one, but a delusion it is, for no obscure member of the House of Commons was ever yet transformed by his parliamentary title into a famous advocate. Nor did the affix of M.P. to the gentleman's name ever promote the lady to a position which was not his and hers by birth already. Mrs. Philander had long since discovered her mistake, had found no pleasure in looking down on her lord from behind the grating in the Ladies' Gallery. Whenever she had ventured on the Terrace she had always retired flushed, secretly wretched, and openly indignant at the ostentatious efforts of Mrs. Ponsonby - Jones, long enthroned as the Terrace Queen, to patronize the new-comer.

When, therefore, Mr. Philander began to keep unhallowed hours, seldom coming home till morning, sometimes not even returning then, but sneaking in with a guilty and disreputable look about lunchtime, saying that he had been forcibly detained by the Whips at an all-night sitting, Mrs. Philander shared the opinion of the peer Premier that the House of Commons was a thing of which one might easily have too much.

II.

NO BETTER THAN A *CAFE CHANTANT*

If Mrs. Philander had a failing it was an over-readiness to listen to the evil whispers of the green-eyed monster. Mr. Theodore Philander was perhaps no better than most of his sex. He was certainly no worse. His wife ought to have seen that when a City senator, Mr. Multiple, who sometimes visited them, seemed with odious familiarity to be rallying Philander on some little incident of no very domestic kind, that gentleman was not merely sinning against taste, but was deliberately playing the part of a mischief-making Iago. But, like most wives who give place to suspicion before they cultivate intelligence, Mrs. Philander, putting, as she expressed it, two and two together, came, as is the habit of ladies with her temperament, to the conclusion that they made not four, but five. The next time, therefore, that her Theodore returned from St. Stephen's at an unholy hour to his South Kensington home with the usual account of detention by Irish or English obstructives, Mrs. Philander plainly let her lord see that she had heard that excuse too often to believe it, openly hinted at returning to her mother, and mentally vowed that she would herself see what was at the bottom of the business, and bring her treacherous spouse to a proper sense of his misdoings.

L

III.

MRS. PHILANDER'S STRATEGY

The wife of the member for Hilborough had read in the society papers of the flirtations on the Terrace with which, on fine Wednesday afternoons, legislators were in the habit of relieving the monotony of dull debates. The place, as one newspaper critic said, was rapidly being transformed into a Thames-side tea-garden, and might easily become something still less dignified and more objectionable.

Shortly after this, Mrs. Philander tingled with indignation at hearing that, for the convenience of their lady guests, the Representatives of the People had resolved to employ waitresses in neat black uniforms, with coquettishly frilled muslin caps, to hand round the strawberries and the tea. However, it is an ill wind which blows no one good. Mrs. Philander, when her temperament did not interfere with her reason, was a quick-witted little lady, and saw in the announcement of " Waitresses wanted for the House of Commons" just the opportunity which she had so long wanted. She had often played in private theatricals, and knew how to dress and look any part she might take. A few skilful touches with the brush, a little more pallor here or colour there, Mrs. Philander was satisfied that none of her friends would recognize her.

She felt a little nervous on entering the private room at the House of Commons of Colonel Jessamy, the gentleman who had kindly undertaken for his brother-M.P.'s to select the new female attendants. But the sensation soon passed off. Maud Philander was engaged in the name of Sarah

Wilkinson for the tea-room department three days a week during the months of June and July.

IV.

WHAT MRS. PHILANDER DISCOVERED

A few days afterwards Sarah Wilkinson began her duties under the directions of the authoritative and forbidding spinster who had charge of the new waitresses. Most of them, as Mrs. Philander could not but admit, were well-mannered and attractive young women, though not, she complacently reflected, any one of them, her own superior in point of personal attractions. She knew from the looking-glass that the regulation costume of black and white suited her perfectly. She was prepared to find her appearance produce some effect upon the parliamentary tea-drinkers whose needs she was now bustling about to supply.

The first person she served was the City M.P. Mr. Multiple, who looked hard at her, evidently did not recognize her, and seemed half inclined affectionately to pat her chin. The next parliamentarian in want of the non-intoxicating cup was Lord Buxton, the Leader of the Opposition. His lordship had a long, expressionless face, somewhat resembling that of a patrician cab-horse in reduced circumstances, with a general predominance of Norman nose. He was, however, credited with accessibility to the charms of the sex, and visibly relaxed his habitual hauteur of manner when the new waitress, with a piquant ignorance or forgetfulness of his rank, said as she placed a tea-cup on the round table—

" Bread and butter or toast, sir ? "

" If," was Lord Buxton's comment to his colleague, Mr. Newhaven, " we are going to have this sort of thing "—and his lordship perpetrated something which in a lowlier mortal might have been a wink—" we had better call the place Cremorne at once!"

Mrs. Philander could scarcely help over-hearing this, began to be rather impatient, and in an unguarded moment was very nearly asking his lordship or Mr. Newhaven if either of them could tell her where Mr. Philander was.

She soon had the reward of her self-control. In something less than an hour her husband emerged from the Chamber to the stone walk outside fronting the river, not, as Mrs. Philander had expected, to keep an assignation, but simply thirsting for a cup of tea, and eyeing with a look of critical approval the figures in black and white drawn up at this moment in single file under the eyes of the already-mentioned superintendent.

Sarah Wilkinson felt a little agitated and

had a horrible suspicion that she was blushing when she tripped off to execute Mr. Philander's order for iced coffee and brown bread and butter. These modest luxuries were deposited on the little table. The nymph, before hurrying off elsewhere, satisfied herself by a single glance that her husband had not penetrated her disguise, but that he was quite as favourably prepossessed by her appearance as Lord Buxton or Mr. Newhaven had been. While she was yet looking at him under her eyelids, the M.P. took out his pocketbook, placed something crisp in an envelope, and began to write on a scrap of notepaper in pencil.

"The wretch!" said to herself Sarah Wilkinson; "I believe he is going to offer me a five-pound note if I will let him walk home with me after work."

v.

THE DENOUEMENT

The lady, however, though not entirely mistaken, had not, as the sequel will show, divined quite correctly the intentions of the member for Hilborough. When she returned with the brown bread and butter, the senator did, indeed, after having finished his coffee, place by the side of the empty cup an envelope. The new waitress took it up. It was addressed to Mrs. Philander. Retiring presently to read the missive, on opening the envelope there fell out a cheque for five-and-twenty guineas. It was accompanied by no proposal to which a committee of old maids could have taken exception, but by the simple words, " This is what you wanted for the new frock ; go home and read *Othello*."

Mrs. Philander, not naturally of large dimensions, felt smaller than nature had made her, intimated to the superintendent that the new place was not likely to suit her, returned to her South Kensington home, and was never known afterwards to express incredulity when Mr. Philander, as a victim of the House of Commons obstructives, returned to his home with the morning milkman instead of at the sound of the evening muffin bell.

How the House of Commons became a Cycling School

WHAT HAD HAPPENED

CONTRARY to the expectation which might be raised by the sequel of these remarks, the long-threatened New Zealander had not yet brought his sketch-book to Westminster Bridge. The arches of that structure were still intact. Penny steamers still lay off what but the other day was known as the Speaker's Steps. No matter how late the hour, or how busy and populous the floor within, the electric light had ceased to glow in the Clock Tower. Inside St. Stephen's Chapel a frequent ringing might be heard. It was not that of a division bell, but of the bicycle. In plain English, the House of Commons as an edifice survived ; as a legislative institution it had ceased to exist. The following is the manner in which these organic changes had been brought about.

II.

HOW IT CAME ABOUT

No Cromwell had, as might have been imagined, expressed himself about the moral antecedents of the elected law-makers with force rather than politeness. Professor Birrell, more occupied with his Quain professorship than with the purge which, in emulation of the historic one of Colonel Pride, he had often talked of applying to the Chamber, had not instigated the removal of the Speaker's mace, of his chair,

or any other such bauble. In a word,
nothing like a revolution by violence had
taken place. Members, indeed, were still
returned nominally to Parliament. Constituencies continued to exist in name. A
former leader in the House of Commons,
whose metaphysical acumen scarcely fell
short of that quality as embodied in a still
more illustrious predecessor, had entered
into an elaborate argument to show that
though St. Stephen's was at this moment
a cycling school, the existence of the House
of Commons was not terminated, but only
suspended.

Several generations before the date now
spoken of, a Parliamentary and literary
genius of the first order had described the
common-sense of a country whose opinions
were mirrored in its free press as recoiling
in disgust from the imperfect vicariate of
a House of Commons. Even that gifted
person, who foresaw much, did not foresee

the incredibly gradual processes by which a constitutional change had been carried into full, if temporary, effect.

The illuminated had for some time felt that, like the Alexandrian library in the judgment of Caliph Omar, the House of Commons was either unnecessary or dangerous. If its decrees coincided with those of "another place," it was superfluous ; if they contradicted that higher wisdom, then the Popular Chamber must clearly be a source of public mischief. During a long series of years the nation had shown a steadily waning interest in the debates of an Assemblage long since robbed of its oratorical ornaments, now exclusively, and to all appearance irreversibly, controlled by excellent men of business, whose addresses were always clear, but never rose above the board-room level.

By this time the most able representatives of the industry, of the wealth, of the many-sided interests of the trade, of the culture, as well as of the diplomacy of the day, were permanently seated in "another place." Either the Administration of the hour possessed the confidence of the Hereditary Chamber or did not possess it. In the former case the Bills sent up to the Lords from the Commons were passed by the Hereditary Legislators before they went home to dine ; in the latter case those measures were never passed at all. The labours of an entire session were undone often within a few hours.

At first popular opinion was amused. Then it was irritated. Finally it became somewhat impatient and disgusted. In this way it often propounded to itself the question whether an Assembly which was really privy to its own effacement could be worth preserving. By this time the more active and ambitious members of the

House of Commons were either born to
a reversionary interest in a seat in the
Peers, or looked forward to such promotion as to the polite goal of their career.
When one, whether an individual or an
assembly, has ceased to believe in himself, the hour of doom is not far from
sounding.

The Leadership of the House of Commons was now divided between a gentleman
who bred shorthorns or played golf and his
associate who rode bicycles and expanded
empires.   Neither of them, as may be
imagined, could spare very much time from
these grave pursuits to take their places on
the right of the Speaker's Chair.   Both of
them were very smart exponents of the
newest social modes.   Both, as is right for
very clever and successful men, had an intellectual contempt for the dull prosers by whom
they found themselves too often surrounded.
Neither, therefore, passed very much time

in the Chamber. The shorthorn breeder had quite enough to do with interviews with his stocktaker in his private room. The bicyclist was always practising new movements on special machines either in Palace Yard, or up and down Westminster Hall, and through the passages and vestibules of St. Stephen's themselves. Some newspapers had ceased to report Parliamentary debates. Others received handsome subsidies for briefly summarizing the proceedings. What, therefore, more natural than that honourable gentlemen should hurry off to dinner or to other engagements, trusting to the printed reports next day if they wished to acquaint themselves with the arguments of their adversaries.

This usage began to be so generally recognized, that questions asking Ministers whether such and such a newspaper's report of their speech was correct began to swarm upon the notice paper.

In consequence attendance in the Chamber fell off so steadily as to cause the figures constituting a quorum to be reduced, by order of the House, first to twenty, then to ten. Even this modest minimum often proved impracticable. Next some member, boldly recognizing the inevitable, moved that the Chamber should sit only on certain days in the week, and that only during some months of the year.

Both the leaders—he who golfed and he who cycled—had been, when at Oxford, at Christ Church. There they remembered it was bad form for any member of the "house" to wear cap and gown. Equally bad form did they consider it now to be visible whenever a debate was going on. They were entertaining ladies on the terrace at tea. They were smoking in their respective private rooms. The House itself was the last place where anyone would look for them.

M

It was now obvious that so capacious a structure in so convenient a situation ought to be turned to some useful purpose. Dreamy philanthropists advocated its acquisition by St. Thomas's Hospital on the opposite bank of the Thames, then sadly in want of a new wing. More practical people rightly thought some money should be made out of it. The leader who golfed protested a few cartloads of sand and furze bushes would adapt it admirably for young beginners at his favourite game. The Poet Laureate, in a stirring ode, advocated a hippodrome, winding up with a suggestion that Dr. Jameson and his friends should be engaged practically to illustrate the incidents of their ride to Johannesburg. The structural alterations required were found to be too extensive.

At this moment an opportunist member hit upon a happy compromise, conspicuously inspired by the genius of the day. While

the mammas and their daughters were
enjoying light refreshments and listening
to inspiriting music on the terrace, why
should not the floor of the disused Chamber
within be transformed into a kind of gym-
nastic *crèche* for the instruction of small
boys, and perhaps little girls, in that difficult
but most necessary of all arts.   A return
was moved for showing the percentage of
fatal accidents from the two-wheeled iron
horse admittedly caused by imperfect education in that method of locomotion which
had now quite superseded the primitive use
of the feet.

This settled the business.   Suggestions
of convenience coincided with the dictates
of humanity.   A measure proposing that
after a certain date the House of Commons
should be dedicated to purposes more
immediately beneficial to all sections of
the community than those which it at
present served was duly drafted, introduced

by the Leader of the House, and carried through all its stages, with the result which, if it be only temporary, is at least historical.

A Story of the Studio

I.

THE SUSPICIONS OF DEAN STARCH

THE Rev. Cyprian Starch, D.D., had resigned some years ago the deanery of Barchester. He was now living on his very comfortable income in his well-appointed town house, 365, Eaton Square. He had no children of his own, and consequently much unoccupied space in his Belgravian mansion. His sister, the wife of General Tinto, had not long since died in India. Her son, Leslie, a clever lad, with much talent of a not very practical kind and with a delicate constitution, on leaving Cambridge put his name down at the Inner Temple, waited for briefs in his

165

chambers, occasionally visited that portion of the Royal Law Courts reserved for members of the Bar, and even reported cases for a law journal. His chief occupation in court, however, was to draw caricatures on little scraps of paper of counsel, judge, jury, and litigants. From this it will be inferred rightly that Leslie Tinto's abilities were chiefly, if not exclusively, artistic. At last the young man openly renounced the law and let his chambers. He was now an inmate of his uncle's house in Eaton Square. Here his mother on her deathbed had consoled herself with thinking her son's health would receive more attention from her sister-in-law, Mrs. Starch, than in London chambers or lodgings.

The young artist's studio was close by in Ebury Street. His kind relatives could not understand why his painting should not be done beneath the roof where he slept and ate. Young Mr. Tinto had to explain the necessity of certain lights to a working painter. These, it seemed, were obtainable only in a room specially constructed for the purpose. So that every morning after the family breakfast Tinto went off to his studio, generally, though not always, returning to the family dinner. Of late his movements had been uncertain and his hours irregular.

The ex-Dean of Barchester, who during twenty years of his life had been a schoolmaster, did not like the look of things. At his clubs, the Old University in Suffolk Street and the Athenæum in Pall Mall, the reverend gentleman had casually heard certain revelations of studio life which aroused his suspicions.

Concurrently with this, the weekly journal called *The Inquisitor* had, after its usual fashion, created a new sensation by a series of articles, "by our Special Commissioner," under the title of "The Artistic Mysteries of London." In these papers every *atelier* was represented as the scene of orgies in comparison with which the life of the Latin Quarter, as depicted in *Trilby*, was monastic, and the *abandon* of Mabille refined.

Then came a powerful article from Mr. Frank, the editor, summing up the evidence which a stern sense of duty had compelled him to print, and appealing to the legislature to regulate by statute the transactions between painters and their models, especially those of the latter who, like Trilby, sat for, to quote the now classical phrase, "the altogether." If, argued the journalist, the lower creation was protected against the outrages of unlicensed vivisectors, how much more sacred in a Christian country ought to be the female form divine.

When at dinner in Eaton Square the Dean turned the conversation into such channels as these, his nephew affected to make light of it, and assured his relative that it was all a tissue of lying nonsense. But Dr. Starch had not been a schoolmaster for twenty years of his life without being able to detect what was passing in the young man's mind when the colour mounted to his cheeks, and other signs were visible of his being ill at ease.

II.

THE DEAN DETERMINES TO SEE FOR HIMSELF

As a gentleman, the ex-Dean of Barchester disliked the idea of playing the spy even upon one for whose moral welfare he felt himself responsible. He was, however, an uncle, charged with practically paternal duties as well. His nephew might, for all he knew, be contracting habits equally ruinous to his moral well-being, to his spiritual and temporal prospects.

One thing Dr. and Mrs. Starch had both noticed. Leslie Tinto had never asked either of them to visit his studio or to inspect the work which he had in progress, and which he talked of submitting to the Academy judges.

"For all you know, my dear," said Mrs. Starch to her husband, "Leslie may have married already one of those persons—ahem!—models as they are called. If you cannot find time to go to Ebury Street, I certainly will!"

The decision announced in these words imposed a fresh obligation on Leslie Tinto's uncle. Mrs. Starch was a woman of her word. No false delicacy would prevent her from personally examining his nephew's studio. The Dean trembled to think what she might find there. A shudder went down to the lowest button of his gaiters as he conjured up the vision of a personal *rencontre* between the blameless and prudish

Churchwoman and another member of her own sex in the act of sitting for "the altogether," her unbound locks flowing down over the unhallowed shoulders, her spirit perhaps fired by a glass of green Chartreuse.

The Dean, it was plain, owed a duty now to his wife as well as to himself, to say nothing of his dead sister and her unhappy son. He would, therefore, on the first day possible pay Mr. Leslie Tinto a visit in Ebury Street, and with his own eyes ascertain the real purpose of his nephew's visits to, and protracted sojourns in, that neighbourhood.

III.

WHAT DEAN STARCH SAW IN THE STUDIO

Arrived in Ebury Street, Dean Starch, heedless of the remonstrances of the housekeeper who opened the door, insisted on ascending at once to his nephew's apartment, without any previous announcement. Vainly did the good woman say she was not sure whether Mr. Tinto was alone; that he might have his sister with him, or——Dean Starch supplied the omission, and gasping out with a sneer, "A model, I suppose!" with more than decanal agility had in another minute flown upstairs and gained the landing just outside Mr. Tinto's studio.

Here the very reverend gentleman paused for a moment. It now struck him that for an ex-dignitary of high degree in the Church of England it would be rather a derogatory and indelicate situation if he entered the room only to be confronted by what he suspected. While he waited at the door he could distinctly hear the voice of his relative in a tone of caress and blandishment within.

"Sit up, my pretty one; you are looking

perfectly divine. Your head a little more towards the light, and bend the body a little to the left."

"Lucky for her that my poor sister did not live to witness the degradation of her son. But I must stop this while I can."

With these words the ex-Dean of Barchester gave a sharp rap at the door in order that the infamous creature might have time decently to drape herself and retire. In a few seconds his shameless nephew invited the caller to "come in." These words were scarcely out of the young man's lips when the Dean heard what he could swear was the smack of a kiss, and the words addressed to the creature within, "We are interrupted, my pet; so put on your rags, and no more for to-day."

In another moment the Dean had entered the studio. The scene which he witnessed spoke for itself. What was it? Unabashed before his easel stood Leslie Tinto, giving a few touches to a female figure on the canvas designed to represent Andromeda liberated from the dragon by Perseus. On a very old easy-chair lay a shapeless mass of drapery, and, as it appeared to the Dean, human limbs dismembered from the body. Leslie Tinto noticed an expression of perplexed disgust on the ecclesiastical face, and astounded the Dean by saying—

"I see you don't know what has become of my pretty one!"

"Sir," replied Dr. Starch, quivering with suppressed fury to the lowest point of his small-clothes, "do you dare to speak of your goings on in this way, and to a clergyman?"

So far from being abashed, the young man broke into a particularly merry laugh, but said nothing. In another minute the young artist took up the *disjecta membra* from the couch. These, with a little dexterous manipulation, presently and, as it seemed to Dr.

Starch, by some act of creative magic, assumed the appearance of a female figure very imperfectly draped

"Now, missy," audibly soliloquized the young man, addressing the dummy whom he had placed in a sitting posture, "sit there by yourself and show the Dean what a well-behaved young lady you are."

Dr. Starch had not felt so small since an audacious boy at Radley, one day before breaking up, had set a butter slide for him, tripping him up in the big school.

"A most ingenious contrivance, my dear Leslie," were the only words the good man could gasp out; "but really, the affection with which you address this inanimate effigy seems a little mysterious, not to say irrational. Why don't you paint, as I believe artists find it necessary to do, from the life?"

"Models, my dear sir," was the reply, "are a luxury I cannot yet afford."

" Let me know the cost, and I will see what I can do for you."

With these words the ex-Dean of Barchester quitted the room, feeling that he had placed himself in a situation altogether unworthy of the clerical rank which he had once held.

The first time that Leslie Tinto had the benefit of "the altogether" for his picture of " Perseus and Andromeda," hung at the next Burlington House show, Dr. Starch provided the model's fee.

How I became Bishop of Barum

REASONS FOR PREPARING THIS NARRATIVE

SO many misstatements concerning my earliest mitre have not only passed into newspaper circulation, but have become partially stereotyped by the flimsy though widely read memoirs of the period, as to make it a duty to the Prime Minister, Mr. Porphyry, who first brought my name before her Gracious Majesty, as well as to myself and my family, briefly to narrate the incidents which caused the then Premier to decide on my succession to the late Dr. Bumbledore in the diocese that I have now held more than a quarter of a century.

II.

With much regret I have seen it stated
that the sermon wherein Mr. Porphyry did
me the honour to discover merit was
preached on a ceremonial occasion, such as
the Judge's Sunday at an assize town, or in
a cathedral in the sister kingdom while the
British Association for the Advancement of
Science was visiting the place.   There is
not the slightest truth in any of these
stories.   I addressed from the pulpit neither
the savants of the empire, nor the scarlet
and ermined executors of justice, nor ever
preached in any cathedral church till I did
so in my own.

Not only did such occasions at no time
fall to my lot: I have always purposely
avoided them.   After twenty years' clerical
labour in various cures, I received from my

noble friend, the patron of the living, the rectory of Otterbourne.

Lord Otterbourne was, I need scarcely say, created a peer by Mr. Porphyry, who had also recommended him to the Queen for the Garter. That these honours were bestowed on my noble friend by the Premier of the day in recognition of his countess's, rather than his lordship's, services to the political party led by the Right Honourable Plotinus Porphyry is notoriously true, for his lordship never personally distinguished himself except at Cambridge by his strange taste to take a part in any " black jobs," in undertaker's phrase, which might be going on. If the premiership of England were open to the fair sex, the honour long since would have been won by her lady-ship (I am not quite sure whether the same thing might not also be said about the primacy itself), for Lady Otterbourne's vigour and versatility of intellect could

compare with any of the historic queens
of her own sex from her of Sheba, or
Zenobia of Palmyra, down to our own
Elizabeth. That Lady Otterbourne ever
supplied with her own pen the pulpit with
any of those sermons which she heard
from the family pew in Otterbourne
Church, as well as prepared her lord's
speeches in Parliament, is, to the best of
my knowledge, a fiction. She was, however,
an accomplished theologian; she would
sometimes to favourite curates suggest
indirectly subjects, and even texts, for
sermons. But obviously this is quite a
different thing from offering these hints to
the rector of the parish. That early in the
week during which Mr. Porphyry was to
be the guest at Otterbourne Hall I received
timely notice of whom my next Sunday's
congregation would contain, together with
the invitation to dinner, is of course the
simple fact.

Mr. Porphyry's vacation pastime was unlike most of those which English statesmen have affected. He neither owned racehorses nor rode to hounds; he did not shoot or fish; he never captained his county eleven; he wrote no articles for the reviews. Unlike his rival, Mr. Petherton, he collected neither bric-à-brac nor old china. Physically, not less than mentally, he was a man of great power. His thews and muscles found the exercise needful to keep them in good order, not in teaching his villagers cricket, as he could have done—for he had been a famous bat—but in lopping the redundant forest growths in and near the grounds of Hazeldene Manor, where he dwelt.

In other words, Mr. Porphyry was the most famous amateur woodman of his day. Whenever, in his own demesne or elsewhere, he noticed any particular elm, or beech, or fir occupying more than its due share of space or light, and thus interfering with the growth or vitality of its fellows, it was with Mr. Porphyry the work of a moment to produce his favourite axe, to take off his coat, to strip himself to the waist, and by as many well-directed strokes as were wanted to remove the superfluous or mischievous branches, in some cases to divide the parent stem itself. The chips that fell to the ground during this process in the days of Mr. Porphyry's greatest popularity, when his newspapers hailed him as " The People's Plotinus," were pounced upon, quick as thought, by his admirers, were privately treasured by them as relics, or were sent as almost sacred curiosities to the local museum.

Mr. Petherton had lately made irreverent fun of these usages; had discovered an untoward analogy between his great rival's favourite amusement and his parliamentary statesmanship, destructiveness, as he said, being the chief characteristic of both. Mr.

Petherton had further cruelly suggested that to form a company for collecting the fragments of bark, even the grains of sawdust shed by Mr. Porphyry's hatchet, and to distribute them at a price to his worshippers throughout the world, would be an excellent plan for raising the funds which the Porphyry party then wanted for their organization. A general election was approaching, when it was announced that the Prime Minister was about to visit Otterbourne Park. He had not been actually defeated in the House of Commons, but the majority in favour of the Minister's local government reforms had become either so diminutive as to lack moral authority, or so out of hand as to be useless. The particular measure which the Minister had pledged himself to pass into law was such an extension of his favourite principle of " devolution " as would make each county, or group of counties, its own paramount authority. Mr. Porphyry's

enemies of course raised the cry of the
ancient monarchy and Parliament in danger
of disintegration. The Minister, however,
ingeniously maintained in answer that, so far
from weakening the Crown or the Imperial
Council, the machinery of his measure, by
pruning away mischievous excrescences and
inspiring municipalities with a new and lofty
sense of their responsibilities, would stimu-
late the sense of loyalty to the legislative
authority at Westminster and to the
sovereign lady upon the throne.

III.

THE SERMON

That the prospect of Mr. Porphyry's
presence at our next Sunday's service
should have been mentioned in conversation between Lady Otterbourne and
myself is very natural. This, however,

I feel sure, was all. I had resolved to
choose a topic which would suggest no
controversial issues, but which, description
being a strong point with me, should admit
of illustration from natural objects familiar
to my parishioners and all who heard my
words. The Otterbourne country is remarkable for the beauty of its woodlands
and the symmetry of the individual trees
composing them. How had this picturesque perfection been obtained? Surely
by the industry of man seconding all the
advantages of nature. Unless the woodman's axe had removed obstructive growths,
and preserved a free passage for air and
sunshine to each member of the plantation
or forest, Lady Otterbourne's trees would
not be, as they justly were, the pride of the
county. In search of an appropriate text
from Holy Writ to introduce these thoughts,
I was struck by a remarkable phrase in the
fifth verse of Psalm lxxiv. These are the

words which describe a man as "famous according as he had lifted up axes upon the thick trees."

I was told afterwards—for when in the pulpit I see nothing—that on hearing the words relating to his favourite craft the Prime Minister lifted up his eyes with a look of surprised intelligence.   Really, it struck me afterwards, if the sacred volume had been searched for a personal prophecy of Mr. Porphyry at his favourite pastime, language more verbally appropriate could not have been found.   The parallel between forestry and other kinds of human action suggested by the above was necessarily now maintained from the pulpit.   Discreet destruction up to a certain point was the necessary condition of good constructive work.

This truth was, with chastened picturesqueness, exemplified by me from the native woodlands of our own Otterbourne,

which assuredly would never have presented
the beautiful appearance they did to-day
unless they had been tended lovingly and
trimmed discreetly by those who have
studied the nature and knew the needs of
sylvan development. The application of
these principles was obvious. I need not
pursue it in detail here, because the dis-
course itself was printed and published at
the request of my parishioners, dedicated,
if I remember rightly, to the Countess of
Otterbourne. As we walked in the park
after service, her ladyship took an opportunity of saying in tones meant for my ears
alone—

"When you talk with Mr. Porphyry at
dinner to-morrow, pray be careful, my
friend, to say nothing which can spoil or
weaken the effect of what we have all been
edified and charmed by hearing from the
pulpit."

I took her ladyship's advice, and such

conversation as I had with the Premier was rigidly confined, I think, to the subject of diocesan colleges for candidates for Holy Orders.

That, however, did not prevent my receiving, a few weeks later, an intimation from the Prime Minister of the pleasure he proposed to do himself in recognizing my thirty years of "unobtrusive parochial labour" by recommending me to her Majesty for the vacant diocese of Barum.

The days have passed when legislation, whatever its subject-matter, can be greatly helped or hindered by the temper of the peers. I shall, however, in conformity with the principles already expressed, have no difficulty in defending the Ministerial local government measure, profanely called the Heptarchy Bill, if it comes up to our House next session, which, as the issue of the elections remains very uncertain, is, to say the least, doubtful. I shall speak as well as vote for it, and shall trust my example may not be without effect on my spiritual and temporal brethren.

The Prime Minister's Love Affair

I.

THE TWO POLITICAL FRIENDS

"REMOTE, unfriended, melancholy, slow." Such was the quotation popularly applied to the frigid and shy Mr. Wenham, who, at the age of thirty-five, had become Prime Minister of England. Tall, upright in figure, with intellectual forehead and firmly-set lips, Wenham gave the House and the public the impression of a man who, for real greatness of character, wanted only a little more imagination. Of late years he had somewhat mellowed, and had unbent himself at dinner-tables and in drawing-rooms more frequently than he

190

had ever yet been known to do. Still his social acquaintances were few; his real intimates were almost none. Ladies, since the death of his wife, he shunned entirely. Of his own sex, he had only one friend. This was Theophilus Wynne, also an M.P., as well as a contrast in every respect to the austere Wenham. A ruddy, jolly face; a figure inclined to rotundity; a good-natured but very knowing smile—these were the salient features of the Premier's genial and life-enjoying confidant.

The political squibs of the period, prose and verse, especially the latter, constantly contrasted the habits, appearances, and tastes of this Nisus and Euryalus of political life. Matron or maid, so sang the social bards, the grave Mr. Wenham was blind to all their charms, deaf to all their blandishments. Not so, the poet proceeded, the gay Wynne.

> "Some like the light, the dark, the short, the tall;
> Not so this statesman. Faith! he loves them all."

That he might the better devote himself to his distinguished friend, Theophilus Wynne, a widower, as was Wenham, abstained from promoting any lady to the vacant place at the head of his table. On the other hand, he expected that his chief should practise a like self-denial. He had, in fact, long since arrived at the conclusion that national interests required Wenham to wed no other wife than his country. More openly he protested that only one lady worthy of Wenham had ever existed. As she happened to have been dead some centuries, and history told of no descendants of Queen Boadicea in the female line, the prospects of a Mrs. Wenham in Downing Street were necessarily rather remote.

Persons who knew nothing of human nature wondered at the intimacy to which the commonplace and epicurean Wynne was admitted by his chief. There was,

however, no mystery in the fact. Wenham
was very busy, and naturally shy. His
nervous energy was not great. He found
conversation when he was not inclined to
it a tax. But he was by no means devoid
of social instincts. No man was more
fitted by nature to be the happy head of
a household, surrounded by a smiling wife
and children at play. Death had deprived
the statesman of the gratification of these
instincts.

Wynne, who had known the Prime
Minister's short and happy married life,
recollected how in those days the austere
and retired Wenham was in the bosom
of his family the most playful and joyous
of men. Directly the grave had closed
over all that was dear to him, Wenham's
inmost nature, as well as his exterior,
changed. His temper became autocratic.
He centred himself so exclusively in political
life that the rest of the world, so far as he

o

noticed it, might as well not have existed. But there were moments when the Minister felt a craving for converse with one of his fellow-creatures. Wynne was the most easily accessible of these. His society placed no kind of strain on the Minister, who could doze in his chair or sit silent as the Sphinx without giving his faithful retainer the slightest offence. One of the statesman's chief amusements was the taking of long country drives, often to a very considerable distance from London, when the cares of state let him be absent for hours, days, even an entire week, as the case might be. In this way the two politicians had traversed much of the home counties, especially Surrey, always incognito, sometimes only recognized by chance visitors at the wayside hotels where they stopped. On such an occasion as this, a new arrival at the chief inn at Guildford, where the pair had passed the night, congratulated an unsuspecting landlord on the distinguished guests he had entertained.

"I don't know," the man replied, "anything about First Lords or Secretaries of the Treasury. All I know is, the stout one, directly they came here yesterday afternoon, made me put three bottles of my best champagne in ice, that afterwards he ordered, to take with his filberts, the best port to be had in the county of Surrey, and that when he paid it this morning he never looked twice at the bill. Them's the politics for me. I have always gone yellow before, but bless me if I don't vote green now to the end of my life!"

II.

MR. WYNNE'S SUSPICIONS

Mr. Wenham found it convenient to be a member of the Centurion Club, so called, not from any military associations, but from the fact of its having first consisted of a hundred members and being domiciled in a Mayfair street in a house indicated by that same number. It was not used by its habitués for dining purposes.

Its life began when other institutions had closed. All the small talk of the town was fumigated by its midnight tobacco. From this haunt Mr. Wynne returned to his bachelor's box in Cleveland Row more discomposed than he was usually seen.

Mr. Wenham, so the talk of the place ran, had at last determined to take a Mrs.

Wenham to himself if for no other reason than to be emancipated from Mr. Wynne. Wynne, of course, treated the report as a joke, perhaps did not believe it himself. But he had more than once observed his chief at receptions in the society of the young lady with whom the statesman's name was now associated. He recalled in Lady Charlotte Fitzhugh a certain likeness to the departed Mrs. Wenham. As he knew that only the force of contrast had socially attracted his patron to himself, so it seemed just possible that the suggestion of a vanished face might really cause Lady Charlotte to captivate a premier.

About this time, too, he knew Mr. Wenham had more than once accepted invitations to friends' houses where he would be likely to meet the clever and attractive young lady, who, with her widowed mother, lived at no great distance from Wynne's own abode.

"If," he soliloquized, "there should be anything in this—and strange things do happen—I really must" (and here Wynne examined complacently his reflection in a looking-glass) "marry her myself."

The more Mr. Wynne thought about the matter, the deeper became his conviction that a benedict Prime Minister was inconsistent with a Prime Minister whose glories were in some way reflected upon Theophilus Wynne, Esq., not a little to that gentleman's satisfaction.

III.

MR. WYNNE'S PATRIOTIC INTERPOSITION

"A remarkably nice young woman, who deserves all the happiness she is likely to get."

Such was the opinion of Lady Charlotte Fitzhugh casually volunteered over the dinner - table to Wynne by the Prime Minister. But the reason for the dismay caused by the remark to the statesman's companion did not end here. The Prime Minister, when he was tired, had a way of letting his words drop without shaping them into deliberate sentences. To complete his amazement, Wynne heard his patron murmur, as if in soliloquy, something of his desire to do what in him lay to contribute to Lady Charlotte's happiness.

Things undoubtedly must be more grave than the Premier's Achates had even supposed. Except, perhaps, with his dinner, Wynne had never been in love in his life. He now noted in the great man's manner the pensiveness conventionally associated with the actual domination of the tender passion.

"What age do you suppose George Damer is?"

Such was the question with which the Prime Minister, apparently apropos of nothing, broke the silence. Remembering to have heard a rumour of Lady Charlotte Fitzhugh's attachment to a Treasury clerk of that name, Wynne, without answering the question, mused to himself on the comparison which he supposed the great man was mentally drawing between his own age and that of a younger rival. Secretly, however, Wynne's resolution was taken. The time evidently had come when he must sacrifice himself in the place of his friend upon the altar of matrimony. If fate had predestined to him a wife, Lady Charlotte Fitzhugh might do as well as another. For himself, he felt no doubt that the Countess of Fitzhugh would welcome as a son-in-law so well placed and highly endowed a gentleman. As for age, "Why," he whispered to himself, "a man is as young as he's feeling; I left off having birthdays at thirty - five, and don't feel more than that now." During the next few days or weeks Mr. Wynne went to more dinner - parties and attended more evening receptions than was his usual habit.

He was more attentive to Lady Charlotte Fitzhugh than he could ever remember having been to anyone who was not a Cabinet Minister. But his main object was to ingratiate himself with the dowager her mamma. That lady, Mr. Wynne noticed, was sometimes escorted into tea-rooms and supper-rooms by a very well-looking young man who had about him the unmistakable cut of the Treasury or the Foreign Office.

"Sir Guy Damer's eldest son, you know, a young man of the most excellent principles and improving prospects, family and official," so Lady Fitzhugh explained the identity of her young cavalier.

On some of these occasions the great Mr. Wenham was himself present, reserved as usual, but evidently, as Wynne thought, with a preoccupied heart. This idea was shared by others. So that patriotism whispered to Mr. Wynne there was no time to lose.

Lady Fitzhugh had casually mentioned she would be at home on a certain afternoon. Wynne arrived, therefore, in Berkeley Square with the certainty of finding her ladyship visible. He had just broken the ice, and was on the point of saying something about "privilege to pay address to charming daughter," when Lady Charlotte Fitzhugh herself entered the room. Taking her mother a little way aside, the young lady, in a voice Wynne could not but overhear, said distinctly—

"That dear, good Mr. Wenham! People

may say he has no heart, but he has made me very happy."

" Great heavens!" mentally ejaculated the Premier's satellite, "so quick about it as this ? "

The next moment the dowager was at his side again, echoing her daughter's praises of the statesman.

What, however, had occurred was this. Mr. Wenham, who, without Wynne's help, had a way of hearing things in which he showed no interest, had learned of the mutual attachment of Lady Charlotte Fitz-hugh and Mr. George Damer. He had also learned that their union was delayed, not by the extreme youth of either, but by the need of some improvement in the gentleman's position.

It so happened that, about this time, the secretaryship of the Tintacks Office had fallen in. Mr. Wenham had at once directed that the offer of it should be made by letter to Mr. Damer, but had reserved to himself the pleasure of personally announcing the fact to Lady Charlotte Fitzhugh.

IV.

HOW MR. WYNNE SAVES HIS FRIEND AND HIMSELF

Mr. Wynne, however much relieved on his own account and his distinguished friend's by the happy turn events had taken, felt nevertheless in a rather awkward position. Happily the declaration to the young lady had been stayed in time. But the fatal secret had been confided to her mother. Nothing remained for Wynne but to assume an air of martyrdom as gracefully as he could.

When, therefore, the dowager said she

awaited Wynne's congratulations, the gentleman assumed a look of sentimental resigna-
tion, remarked with a voice which had a
tear in it that "there were chords, but
that Providence tempered the wind to the
shorn lamb," and that he thought he might
get over the shock.

Nothing less like the gentle animal first
mentioned not by King Solomon, but by
Laurence Sterne, could be conceived than
the well-conditioned figure and smiling,
ruddy face of the Prime Minister's friend.

The dowager, however, did not laugh,
and scarcely smiled as she rejoined—

"Yes, Mr. Wynne! I should not be at
all surprised if your Christian fortitude
does enable you to sustain the blow."

Not very long after these events took
place, a fashionable marriage was celebrated
at St. James' Church, Piccadilly. The bride
was given away by the Prime Minister
himself, whose colleague in office her

father had been. Mr. Wynne, as he said facetiously, the youngest bachelor present, returned thanks for the bridesmaids in a little speech full of pathos and wit.

The happy pair, amid showers of rice and satin shoes, drove off to pass the honeymoon at a Thames-side villa which Theophilus Wynne, Esq., M.P., had kindly lent them for the occasion, and which had witnessed in other days many a pleasant little dinner whereat the proprietor had entertained the Prime Minister, who, by-the-bye, though scarcely yet middle-aged, remains unmarried to this day.

Lord Boscobel's Garter

THE STORY OF A QUOTATION

"Optat ephippia bos piger."—*Hor. Ep.*, i. 14, 43.

I.

MR. PYNSENT, the most autocratic, but also the most popular, Prime Minister whom the Great Green party had produced for fifty years, sat in his library reading, with an expression on his face as of one half puzzled, half amused, a letter, adorned with an earl's coronet, just placed in his hands.

"So Bos is determined not to be too late this time; old Tintagel's hatchment was only up yesterday, and here is this very plain hint about vacant honours.

Palmerston—or was it Melbourne?—liked the Garter because there was no d——d merit about it, but I am sure he never had a Boscobel to bother him."

As he soliloquized thus a childish knock was heard at his door, and the Premier rose to admit and welcome his small visitor. While he is doing this, it may be well to state that Lord Boscobel had, in the darkest days of the Green outship, been a valued and consistent supporter of the party in general and of Mr. Pynsent in particular.

The Prime Minister was not a rich man. Lord Boscobel's wealth, accumulating through a long minority and augmented by the discovery of fresh coal seams, had made him a Plutus among peers. Lord Boscobel was not himself a profound politician, but was a keen party man. The world saw in him only a good-natured, easy-going, rather sleepy aristocrat, fond of his comfort in the first place, pleased to gratify the sense of his own importance by patronising a statesman so eminent as Mr. Pynsent, and as a social pillar of a political organization so much in need of that sort of support as the Great Green party at this time was.

Such an estimate of the nobleman with whom we are now dealing was true as far as it went, and so far as it went only. It entirely left out of account his characteristically patrician thirst for further promotion in the dignity of the peerage. If his lordship's political faith consisted, as indeed it did, of a single article, a faith in Mr. Pynsent's statesmanship, there co-operated with this in his noble mind a belief in Mr. Pynsent as the most convenient instrument for securing his further advancement in the pages of Debrett and Burke. Therefore it was that Lord Boscobel never refused to subsidize any election candidate for whom his chief wrote a letter of recommendation ;

P

that he had placed his yacht at Mr. Pynsent's disposal whenever that statesman was ordered by his doctors to take a sea-voyage. Lord Boscobel's house in Berkeley Square and villa at Richmond were ever at his idol's command when, as of late years had happened frequently, the Great Green leader had chanced to be out of office, and so without a residence of his own in town.

Mr. Pynsent, who went less into society than his predecessor, Mr. Burton, had, unknown to himself, a rival in the affections of Lord Boscobel, Mr. Horace Twining, more familiar to all sections of the polite world of the capital by his simple pagano-Christian name, "Horace." Since their Harrow and Cambridge days, Mr. Twining had lived much with, and even more on, the Earl of Boscobel.

No one exactly understood the secret of his lordship's attachment to Mr. Twining, though the true explanation was exceedingly simple : that gentleman was never in the way and never out of it ; he could foresee by instinct when he was likely to be wanted ; he disappeared and reappeared at the right moment by a dexterous intuition. Horace Twining had the reputation in semi-royal quarters of being companionable ; he was a young man of good address and tact, of some cleverness, and of a great deal more cunning. His position as *âme damnée* to Lord Boscobel had given him prosperity. He superintended, without his presence being felt, the hereditary mansion in Berkeley Square ; he controlled, for their proprietor's good, Lord Boscobel's Welsh collieries, without his managerial hand obtruding itself on their proprietor's presence. Even before the death of Lord Tintagel, the Earl of Boscobel had advanced his pretensions to the Blue Riband, and Mr. Horace Twining, who had reasons of his own for thinking that his noble patron had done enough for the Green connection and for its leader, was not the young gentleman to miss an opportunity of encouraging the idea in the mind of his lordship that he was a peer with a grievance. Mr. Twining's comment upon the whole situation amounted in effect to this :—

"Now that Tintagel has gone, and you have been passed over twice, I should send in my ultimatum."

II.

Long before the time which it has taken me to write this, Mr. Pynsent's visitor had entered, and the Premier's son, a rather clever and a very ubiquitous lower-school Etonian of fourteen, was sitting on a chair close to his father's writing-table. If Mr. Pynsent ruled his party with a rod of iron, his wife, Lady Emily, and his children

controlled him in cords of silk; and one
of the writers in the *Scorpion*, who had,
in a fit of disgust at not finding himself
a lion at Mr. Pynsent's Thames-side villa,
on the occasion of a Saturday to Monday
visit not long since, avenged himself
amicably for this neglect at the hands of
his host by a vicious article, entitled "Small
Boys in Big Houses," which the Prime
Minister had never seen, for though the
great-hearted scribe had sent the paper,
turned down at his chivalrous invective
against Mr. Pynsent's children, the broadsheet had been intercepted by a secretary
and deposited in the waste-paper basket,
so many and impregnable are the lines
of defence which protect Cabinet Ministers
against the irreverent familiarities of the
press.

III.

As Mr. Pynsent indicated by his movements that he was now about to answer the recently received missive of the patrician candidate for the two coveted initials whom he had almost unconsciously spoken of by the familiar monosyllable " Bos," the small boy rose to go.

" No need for you to run away, Percy. This is a letter which you could answer as well as I can with four words of Horace that you learned in the lower fourth."

And with a smile Mr. Pynsent quoted the Horatian example from the Latin syntax, " Optat ephippia bos piger."

Left alone by his sire in the library, Master Pynsent soon began restlessly to contrive some occupation for himself.   His fond father had often told him that some day he should be his private secretary.

"Happy thought!" chuckled the Eton urchin to himself. Why should he not begin his secretarial apprenticeship at once, and show that he could, in his own phrase, "do a little stroke off his own bat" on his father's casual hint? The smart boy saw that his parent had got no further with his reply to the Boscobelian application than to address the envelope to the noble Earl in Berkeley Square. The child seized a pen, and observing a letter lying open in remarkably clear characters, resolved to fashion his own caligraphy after this model. The handwriting that Master Pynsent now made it his object to reproduce happened, as perverse luck would have it, to be the MS. of Mr. Twining himself, a note he had addressed by him to the Premier on his patron's business. "Optat ephippia bos piger," murmured, with self-approval, the

Etonian as, with a fine flourish of his quill,
he finished the classical excerpt, enclosed
the paper adorned with this epigraph in
its envelope, and dropped it into the
receptacle for the postal despatches of the
Premier.   Percy Pynsent hurried off to his
fond mother.

IV.

"Nothing the matter, I hope, Bos?   You
look as if something had upset you."

These were the words which on the day
following the above incident were addressed
to Lord Boscobel by Mr. Oxymel, the most
suave and effective of Treasury Whips, as
the pair met in the morning-room of the
Purple Patch Club, a non-political association in St. James' Street, but much affected
by both parties in the State.

"Something has upset me," abruptly
replied Lord Boscobel, and taking the

Pynsent missive from his pocket-book, he said to Mr. Oxymel, "Can you tell me who wrote this?"

The Whip glanced hurriedly at the Latin words, and said, "Horace, I believe; but I know 'the sage' is in the library, for I saw him talking there to Twining ten minutes ago. To be sure, let us go and ask him; he knows everything."

Among the blind the one-eyed is king, and, with all due respect to the denizens of the joint-stock palaces of London, if one excepts the precincts of that abode of mildly convivial omniscience the Athenæum, a club reputation for universal knowledge is gained somewhat easily.

"*Ce diable Harcourt, ils ait tout,*" was the admiring ejaculation of the French Minister when his private secretary pointed out to him that Melbourne was not, as his chief had fondly imagined, at the Cape, but in Australia.

Mr. Crabbe, above alluded to by his club sobriquet, "the sage," was a retired Indian judge, who, being condemned by dyspepsia to pass the dinner-hour over tea and toast in the club library, indemnified himself for this enforced "sojourn with the silent dead" by seldom saying a good word about the active living. During his residence in a remote Madras station he had kept up some of his Haileybury learning, and he had not yet been long enough at home to lose it all.

"Who wrote that?" asked Mr. Oxymel of the Oriental pundit, placing as he did so the Latin legend received by Lord Boscobel in Mr. Crabbe's hand.

"Why," replied "the sage," judicially surveying the paper through his pince-nez, and looking the while as many unutterable things as he could, "who could have written it but Horace? Somewhere," he added, sinking his voice to a confidential whisper, "in the Epistles or the Satires, but Horace, I know. Any schoolboy would have told you that."

"Exactly what I said to Lord Boscobel just now," commented Mr. Oxymel, for whom the world contained no other Horace but his own special *bête noire*, Mr. Horace Twining.

"And," rambled on "the sage," "curiously enough, another Horace, your friend Mr. Twining, was seated writing at yonder table five minutes ago, and has left there a specimen of his precious penmanship."

This seemed to the Whip too good to be true, but it was a fact nevertheless. Quickly seizing the scrap of paper with its few words of Mr. Twining's MS., he said, "Now, my lord, compare that with what you have in your pocket, and you will see that I am something of an expert after all."

"I have not had much practice in that

sort of thing," rather sulkily rejoined Lord Boscobel to the blithe, jubilant little Treasury understrapper, "but I don't think the classics are much in *our* Horace's line," with which words the peer, visibly nettled, went off to keep an appointment.

"I should not be surprised," observed Oxymel, "if that noble lord were to give our friend Twining a bad quarter of an hour to-morrow morning."

"It would be much more to the purpose," grumpily observed the scholar from Hindostan, "if his lordship were to spend a quiet twenty minutes with his Horace in his library to refresh his classics and improve his mind."

"Good heavens!" exclaimed Oxymel, with a surprised laugh, "I believe we are playing a regular game of cross questions and crooked answers. My dear sage, what 'Horace' do you suppose we are speaking about?"

"The only Horace I care to know," responded the victim of chronic jaundice, who could be as sentimental over his classics as over his curry itself, "is the Venusian bard."

"Oh!" laughed the man of affairs, "you mean the *sabine furin, fons bandusiæ*, and all that sort of thing—I don't believe Boscobel has looked inside a Latin book since he left Harrow. We were talking about a very different thing, Horace Twining's fist."

"I thought," curtly replied Mr. Crabbe, "you asked me who wrote the words about 'bos piger, etc.,' which I fancied someone had rather smartly applied to Lord Boscobel's wish for the Garter. But," he added in a musing tone, "how odd that the handwriting should be so like Twining's."

v.

When, on the day following these conversations at the Purple Patch Club, Mr. Twining presented himself to his patron in Berkeley Square, he found the noble Earl somewhat ruffled in his temper, and disposed to be peremptory in his manner.

While Lord Boscobel was deliberating whether, without too much risk of looking foolish, he could demand an explanation from Mr. Twining at the risk of breaking with his creature, as well as losing the services of a particularly convenient henchman, he was told that the Prime Minister's son was waiting to see him.

The fact is, that since Mr. Percy Pynsent had rejoined his mother on the eventful afternoon above described, a good deal, as they say in the House of Commons, had happened.

"My boy," said Lady Emily Pynsent, when her son had finished the narrative of his epistolary exploit on his sire's behalf, "this is a more serious matter than you ever fancied, and may cause us some inconvenience. It will be a good experience of men and manners for you to get out of your scrape as you best can. Lord Boscobel is good-nature itself, but even good-natured peers may stand upon their dignity, and even your *bos piger* will not like you the better for laughing at him."

"Trust me, my dear mother," were the boy's words, uttered with the sublime self-assurance which belongs to extreme Etonian juvenility, "to put matters straight. I will see," the boy condescendingly added, "Bos myself to-morrow; he is a gentleman, and must accept an apology."

When that night Mr. Pynsent emerged from his dressing-room, Lady Emily said something to him as to the bestowal of

the Garter vacant by the demise of the
Earl of Tintagel ; but with more abruptness
than was usual—for he had just been run
rather too close to be pleasant in a House
of Commons division — the Premier told
his lady that there were at least three names
on his list having precedence over Lord
Boscobel.

"We shall see, my dear," were Lady
Emily's last words as beside her her distinguished spouse, who had the first attri-
bute of statesmanship, the power to sleep
at will, sank tranquilly into the innocent
slumber of the patriot in office.

VI.

Percy Pynsent, though little more than
fourteen, was a thorough man of the world
in miniature, as so many Eton boys are.
Once closeted with Lord Boscobel, the

Premier's son, plunging *in medias res*, began by saying—

"I am awfully sorry, but look here, Bos," he was about to say, but checked himself just before he had uttered the monosyllable by which he was accustomed to hear his seniors speak of the Premier's pet peer, and having finished this brief preface of apologetic regret, the youthful Pynsent added: "I really don't know what made me do it. It didn't strike me," he went on to say, "that *piger* meant lazy. The fact is, I confounded it with what they call Achilles: *impiger, iracundus, inexorabilis, acer.* I thought you would not mind being compared with the fellow who was so good a shot that he could kill anybody by hitting him in the heel running," from which slightly confused explanation it will be seen that Master Pynsent had no very accurate recollection of the Homeric legend. To receive a schoolboy's apologies, however

Q

sincere, when the apologist himself can
only with visible difficulty preserve the
gravity of his voice and face, is not a very
dignified position for a peer of mature
years, and Lord Boscobel caught with
relief the first opportunity of terminating
the interview by slipping a crisp piece of
water-marked paper into the hand of his
caller, and expressing a hope that when the
youth returned from his exeat to his house-
master's in Keate's Lane he would find
the eleven in good trim for the impending
match against Harrow at Lord's.   Whether
Lord Boscobel was or was not immediately
after this decorated with the Blue Riband
left at the Prime Minister's disposal by the
decease of the Earl of Tintagel it is unnecessary to say, but of the following facts
there is no doubt: that at this present
time his lordship has his allotted stall in
St. George's Chapel; that he has shaken
off the inactivity which earned for him his

bovine abbreviation of his patronymic ; that he is now a useful official in Mr. Pynsent's fourth administration ; that he has no longer need of Mr. Horace Twining's services ; that he has lately taken Mr. Percy Pynsent, whose school and college days alike are over, as his " private secretary unpaid," all of which incidents may be referred directly to the Etonian's expedition to his father's library on the fateful afternoon the history and sequel of which have been faithfully set forth here.

The Cabinet Council

THE EDITORIAL COMMISSION

ALL the quidnuncs of Pall Mall, all the oracles of Fleet Street, every editor in the kingdom, London or provincial, knew intuitively that there was a fresh crisis in the Cabinet. So well had the secret been kept, that no conjectures worth a moment's credence had yet been circulated by any of the news-agencies as to its cause. The editor of the *Penny Trumpet*, Mr. Guy Limber, disgusted that the Premier, Lord Courtfield, had not taken him into the Ministerial confidence, had registered a vow to devise means of unveiling the mysteries of State before his paper was many numbers older. Limber united the keen scent of a detective with the fervour of a crusader. His taste might sometimes seem low. His moral purpose was said by those who knew him best always to be high. By his own skilful example and his power of communicating his professional enthusiasm to those whom he employed, in the course of "interviews," so improved by the British adapter as to make the Yankee inventor green with envy, Limber had habituated his public to such artistic accounts of the transactions of the Cabinet at home, or of the deliberations of diplomatists abroad, that the statesmen immediately concerned in the episodes were often highly edified when they read for the first time the *Penny Trumpet's* account of their proceedings. Of the many applicants for service on his staff in business of this sort, the strenuous editor had just chosen one modest youth fresh from college, in whom he thought he perceived great aptitudes for journalistic service. Reginald Dimley had worshipped the great Limber since as an undergraduate he had sent a paragraph of college gossip to the office of the *Penny Trumpet*. He was a gentleman-like, well-connected, and pleasant-mannered lad. His friends had destined him for the Civil Service; but he no sooner perceived the possibility of association with Limber than, discarding all domestic remonstrances, the newly-fledged graduate took employment under the man who more than anyone else he admired. As yet he had not won his spurs in his new occupation. The editor indeed was beginning to doubt whether he might not have misjudged the aspirant. But Dimley was very willing. Limber had the forbearing patience of greatness, and now he thought events might give his contributor a better chance than they had before.

The Premier was to entertain some of his colleagues on a week's-end visit at his seat, Courtfield Castle. It at once occurred to the shrewd editor that as Lord Palmerston held important conferences at Broadlands, so his successor and admirer would utilize the presence of his brother politicians beneath his roof informally, at least, to discuss the grave issues of State with which the hour was big.

Clearly, therefore, the immediate thing to do was for Dimley to travel to Courtfield Castle for a Saturday-to-Monday outing; when there, on some plea or other, to smuggle himself into the First Lord's house, and to trust to luck for picking up an authentic idea of the State business transacted around him. This, then, was the editor's commission to his zealous but very raw and credulous recruit, adding: " I believe that the whole Cabinet trouble is caused by Mr. Jaguar's overbearing ways."

Dimley thought he would have no difficulty in effecting an entrance into the Castle where the great men were to foregather. Fortune favoured him more than he had hoped. He knew something at college of a son of the Premier's. When, at the club to which they both belonged, Dimley mentioned casually that on such and such a day he would be walking with his knapsack not far from Courtfield, Lord Henry Courtfield amiably said that he hoped the young journalist would receive a note asking him to pass the night beneath his father's roof.

The little pedestrian tour which Dimley had suggested was struck out of his programme, and at the close of the week the young man presented himself at the main entrance of Courtfield Castle. He was received at the front door by a magnificent gentleman whom he took to be the noble host himself, and with whom, in a moment of nervous impulsiveness, he was about to offer to shake hands. The mistake was not committed, for at this moment Lord Courtfield himself appeared on the scene. Noticing that the young man looked hot and tired and shy, he said to the stately being who had so awed the new-comer—

"Jarman, show Mr. Dimley his room— the Blue Room, next to the Cabinet Chamber—and see whether he would like to have a cup of tea brought to him!'

Courtfield Castle had been in the Premier's family for centuries. Most of its rooms were distinguished by some historic title, *e.g.*, the Star Chamber, or the Queen's Boudoir, or in the present case the Council Chamber, where our young friend was to be domiciled for the night. But Reginald Dimley, full of visions of statesmen in secret conclave assembled to settle high questions of State, did not think of this, and could only congratulate himself on being so close to the scene of the Ministerial deliberations.   Not, of course, that he would have turned eavesdropper.   But sometimes, you know, it is impossible not to overhear things, however one may dislike it.

II.

THE CABINET AT WORK

While the young journalist was refreshing himself with his tea he heard a light tap at his door, and Percy Courtfield, the Premier's son, to whom he owed his invitation, entered—a simple, ingenuous youth, who only wished to make the visitor at his ease, and who knew how servants in great houses sometimes bully guests to whose comfort they do not think it will be profitable to minister.

"Be sure," were the words of the Premier's son to his acquaintance, "to ask for all that you want, and to see that you get it. The fact is," he continued, "there is something like a civil war downstairs in this house going on. Jarman, the groom of the chambers, whom you saw loafing about in the hall as if all the place belonged to him just now, makes himself so confoundedly disagreeable to the under-servants that they will do nothing if they can help it, and visitors are left to look after themselves."

Left alone by his friend once more, Dimley began mentally to deliberate how his present position in the ministerial dwelling was to be turned to newspaper account. He could not, he reflected, with decency thus early in his visit put any leading questions to his host, and the Ministers who might be beneath the same roof as himself were not likely to volunteer him any important statements. While these thoughts occupied him he could hear, with a plainness which surprised him, the click of billiard balls, and the voice of someone marking the game :—

"Plain, sixteen, spot, twenty-four, and six to go up."

Evidently the partition walls of Courtfield Castle were not thick. In a few more seconds Dimley was roused from his reverie by the sound of several footsteps unmistakably just outside his door.

"Evidently," he said to himself, "Ministers are now just entering the Council Room, next to which Lord Courtfield said I was to be. If these walls are all so thin, who knows what I may be compelled, however much against my wish, to hear?"

Almost mechanically Reginald Dimley took out his notebook and spread it on the table before him, so as to be prepared for all contingencies.

"I'm not a-goin' to stand this bloomin' sort of thing any longer! I've not a word to say against his lordship or the place ; but if this new-comer, who is put over us all, is to treat us like so much dirt, I shall resign my place."

Other voices followed to the same effect, all polite enough about Lord Courtfield, but bitterly discontented against the beggar on horseback who, in the phrase overheard by Dimley, had been put over them all. Dimley remembered his editor's theory of Mr. Jaguar as the cause of the Cabinet trouble, and chuckled at receiving such direct confirmation of the view.

Presently the conversation ceased.

"Evidently," said Dimley to himself, "the Council is over now. I had no idea that Cabinets only lasted so short a time, and that noble statesmen used such low slang.

However, the situation is quite clear, and I have been compelled to hear enough to make it plain that a powerful section of the Cabinet kicks against Jaguar having his way so much, and they don't mince matters about it either. Really, their disgust with him almost makes them forget their good manners."

III.

THE DESPATCH PREPARED

It had during many weeks been an open secret that the Stalwarts of the Light Green party were displeased at the ascendency over the consultations of the Cabinet which the energetic Secretary of State, Mr. Jaguar, had acquired. He had been introduced into the Cabinet by the Premier to conciliate an important body of popular supporters. On the strength of this fact he really claimed to

control its policy, much as Dimley had heard the political malcontents in the adjoining compartment describing.

All this our journalist had time enough before the dinner-bell rang to put into a crisp, piquant narrative of the Ministerial situation, written for immediate despatch to the editor of the *Penny Trumpet*. Reginald Dimley was finishing his article, when there came another tap at his door. Once more it was young Courtfield, who again expressed a hope that the literary visitor had received all proper attention.

" My father has himself noticed," he added, "that groom of the chambers, Jarman's, bullying ways with the other servants. They have made a very proper representation to him about it, and I hope it will end in Jarman's going. By George! I can hear his horrid voice in that room on the other side of you."

" You don't mean," returned Dimley,

"that the man is in the same room as the Cabinet Ministers?"

The Premier's son could not restrain an amused laugh.

"I see," he said, "you are misled by the name; but it has no more to do with the Cabinet than with the Spanish Inquisition. It is called so just to distinguish it, instead of giving it a number as they do in hotels. Who used it in Queen Elizabeth's days I don't know. Now it is a sort of still-room. No one ever goes inside it except the upstair servants."

Poor Reginald Dimley cast a look of touching regret at the manuscript which he had just completed, and had been, indeed, about to post to his chief. Of course, the whole thing was plain now. But though the composition just completed was not to go to the office for which it had been prepared, the contributor's visit to Courtfield Castle was not destined to be without result.

Lord Courtfield, a kind-hearted man, who sympathized with newspaper writers, especially if they supported him, as the staff of the *Penny Trumpet* did, complimented in the course of the evening the young journalist, his guest, on certain compositions which he had read, and then, with frank good humour and an amused laugh, said—

"Perhaps before you return to town you would like to know the truth about these rumoured dissensions in the Cabinet?"

Dimley's face at once brightened, only, however, to be overcast when the Prime Minister continued—

"About that I can say nothing, because," he added, with a twinkle in his eye, "there are no dissensions to talk about."

Before Reginald Dimley went to bed he composed another article, embodying his real interview, just recorded, with Lord Courtfield, but necessarily, as the phrase is, somewhat "exploiting it." On this the

R

Penny Trumpet's editor based a powerful leading article, cautioning the public against "the mischievous inventions of eavesdropping contemporaries." Although, therefore, Dimley's smartly-written original account of the situation had been committed to the flames by its author, the young man, on getting back to his newspaper office, found that his position with his chief was even better than if the narrative of what he had imagined to take place in the Cabinet Room of Courtfield Castle had actually been despatched and published with all the honours of leaded type.

The "Whitechapel Wonder"

A STORY OF THE NEW JOURNALISM

I.

THE GENESIS OF THE IDEA

THE great colonial capitalist Nathaniel Knapp, a middle-aged gentleman with a bull-neck and rather an apoplectic appearance, was entertaining at supper in his chambers in the Albany a guest whom he was in the habit of playfully indicating by the name of "my friend the clergyman." His guest's ecclesiastical robes consisted of a splendid silk gown trimmed with chinchilla fur and a magnificent sealskin cloak, now thrown carelessly aside on the tapestry-covered couch. In place of the tonsure the divine wore a sumptuous growth of real auburn hair. The complexion, brilliant, if at moments a trifle too florid, told of anything but ascetic vigils of prayer. The clergyman's name, as given soon after birth, was Cherry Wilkins. Since then it had been glorified into Cherubina Willoughby. The salary commanded by the owner of this *nom de théâtre* amounted to a large slice out of the income attached to an Anglican canonry.

The ostensible occasion of the present meeting between the ex-member for Melbourne, who, having sheared a thousand flocks, had now thoughts of becoming member for London, and the clerical object of his Platonic attachment, was to settle preliminaries for enabling Miss Cherubina Willoughby (*née* Sally Wilkins) "to go into management" on her own account. That highly endowed and remarkably

shrewd lady had, however, been thinking
over the idea ; had come to the conclusion
that the West End possessed quite as many
theatres as it could support already, and
that the philosophic appreciator of the
" Queen of the Variety Stage " might, rather
more to that sovereign's advantage, invest
his money in a different quarter.

The skeletons of the ortolans had been
removed by Nathaniel Knapp's valet.
Turning the chair round from the table to
the fire, the ecclesiastic known in the playbills by the style already named permitted
the devoted colonial to place one of his
perfumed cigarettes between her lips and
then to light it.

The following was the substance of what
the divine skirt-dancer and incomparable
mimic (see " Frivolity's " nightly playbills)
had to say. This fair and prudent person,
having been thinking things over, had come
to the conclusion that there was, in the new

slang, a "slump" in theatres and a boom in newspapers.

"Why not," was the upshot of her suggestion, "run an evening paper of your own?"

This would at once advance the professional interests of Miss Cherubina Willoughby and help the social and political aspirations of Nathaniel Knapp. Was not the *Mayfair Butterfly* for sale?

"Suppose you buy that, and either," added Miss Willoughby, "edit it yourself, or get a real man about town, like Wallace Caroll, none of these Fleet Street hacks, to edit it for you?"

Knapp, seeing that his "clerical friend" had already settled the question mentally, had no thought of serious resistance, and only said, as a mere matter of form, that he understood nothing of newspapers.

"No more," commented Miss Willoughby, "do you of theatres. You can get all the

business done for you. I will see you are
not cheated, and everyone knows that an
evening newspaper is the *chic* thing to have
nowadays."

II.

THE "WHITECHAPEL WONDER" STARTED

If playhouses were at a discount, so, as
he lay awake that night considering the
subject, must also, it struck Nathaniel
Knapp, be newspapers, *ante* or *post
meridian*. If the thing was to be done at
all, the first essential was to strike out a
new and original line. Any plant or goodwill which the *Mayfair Butterfly* possessed
might possibly be worth buying if it were

to be had cheap. But as for the title, Knapp would have nothing of that.

Determining at once to "go for" something which would secure attention by mere force of repulsion and shock, the ingenious Knapp, as if by sudden inspiration, repeated aloud to himself the words, "*The Whitechapel Wonder*, with which is incorporated *The Mile End Mercury*, a paper of two worlds."

Knapp's remarkable successes during his colonial career had persuaded him that nothing which he touched could fail. Above all, he would give a wide berth to professional journalists, whom he knew to be an impecunious, and whom he, therefore, chivalrously concluded to be, in his own words, "a low lot."

The *Mayfair Butterfly* had excellent offices in the western section of the Strand; the paper, premises in Salisbury Street, accommodations, and goodwill were, as

Miss Willoughby had assured him, to be bought at a bargain. Mr. Wallace. Caroll knew as little of printers' ink and editors' measuring rule as Nathaniel Knapp himself could desire.

On the other hand, Caroll had contributed to the daily and weekly press in days gone by; had received a good education, which he had not quite forgotten ; was supposed to know the world, and to be well received at the illustrious dwelling which adorns the south-western extremity of Pall Mall.

Mr. Caroll received the proposal, not indeed aridly, but still favourably. He had some sense of humour, which was gratified by the idea of a *Whitechapel Wonder* whose offices were almost within a stone's-throw of his own St. James's Street club, and whose editor was one of the most universally requested men at the West End. Of course Mr. Knapp would understand that for undertaking the work Caroll would need, not only a handsome salary, but a capable coadjutor.

"That," promptly responded Knapp, "the proprietor of the *Whitechapel Wonder* had seen to already."

The next day, therefore, the new owner of the West End journal with the East End name introduced to his chief editor, Wallace Caroll, his future Adlatus, Mr. Shirley Brabazon, resembling his titular chief in his ignorance of everything to do with newspaper technique, but in nothing else. Wallace Caroll was a short, dapper little gentleman, with a tendency to *embonpoint*, with a moist, merry, twinkling eye, the largest fund of good anecdote in the United Kingdom, and a native inability to take existence seriously. Equally popular in the region of green-rooms and of princely habitations, he was a particular favourite (*bien entendu*) of the "Queen of the Variety

Stage," the "Empress of European Skirt-dancers," Miss Cherubina Willoughby herself.

On the other hand, the collaborator of the ex-diplomatist Caroll, Mr. Shirley Brabazon, a tall, severe figure of sallow, saturnine countenance, was a very serious person indeed. In earlier life an ascetic student, he had been associated prominently with the Puseyite movement, and had, in fact, taken Anglican orders. Though long since he had taken advantage, like other eminent men, of the parliamentary Act enabling him to doff his priestly calling, the deportment and traditions of the priesthood still clung to Brabazon. His favourite studies were mediæval architecture and Greek Church theology. Quite recently the majestic Miss Maud Mammoth, the greatest tragedienne of two hemispheres, was said to have touched a tender chord in the bosom of the austere Brabazon. Be that as it may, this much is certain: whenever the Mammoth's name was in the bill, Brabazon was seldom now out of the house. Whether this was all none could say. For the colleague of Caroll was about as communicative as an oyster, and when he turned his back upon the dinner-table left no more track behind him in his going than a spider promenading on the sea-sand.

III.

HOW THE "WHITECHAPEL WONDER" PROSPERED.

When, punctual to the stroke of 10 a.m., the editors of the *Whitechapel Wonder* alighted at their office door in the little street out of the Strand, the children and servant-girls of the precinct were on the look-out to be cheered by a smile from Caroll, or withered by Brabazon's scowl. If, as sometimes happened, the twin conductors undertook the management of the paper on alternate days, there was as much or as little of resemblance or consistency between the principles on which the two successive issues of the journal were compiled as if they had been numbers of *The Sporting Life* and the *Church Times* respectively. This at least secured variety, but did not always please the proprietor, and tried the public.

No serious collision resulted from this diversity of temperaments and styles, except when the time came to comment on the social fashions or foibles of the day. If the writer retained by Brabazon to denounce the frivolities of the contemporary stage was rather too rough upon the accomplishments in which Miss Willoughby excelled, particularly upon skirt-dancing and mimicry, or referred rather pointedly to the impersonations of Miss Mammoth as alone redeeming the contemporary boards from absolute worthlessness, Wallace Caroll the next day applied the needful corrective to such sour doctrines by inserting an article "from our special critic" on the moral tendency of Miss Willoughby's performances, or an ode "from our newest poet laureate" apostrophizing that lady's gyrations as the poetry of motion. In this way the balance was held pretty equally, and the boat sailed, on the whole, with an even keel.

There were, of course, other contributors to the *Whitechapel Wonder* besides Caroll and Brabazon, who, as a matter of fact, wrote very little with their own pens, that they might the better perform the editorial function of guiding the pens of others.

While the public was, on the whole,

amused by the daily and unforeseeable mutations of the print, which had, of course, won the nickname of *The Strand Weathercock*, to the contributors and generally to the well-wishers of the paper the system had its inconveniences. Those letters from outraged correspondents to the editor provoked by the tactics of Wallace Caroll were, if they reached the office when his colleague was on duty, wholly ignored by Shirley Brabazon, and *vice versâ. Laissez aller*, when reduced to a system after this fashion on an evening newspaper, has its disadvantages.

The various writers of articles and of "notes" began to complain when they found the arrangements to which Caroll had pledged the proprietor absolutely ignored by Brabazon. As it proved impossible to secure attention and redress under the newspaper's dual control, the journalists employed on it, or the members of the public particularly offended by its vagaries, applied directly to the proprietor, Nathaniel Knapp, who wished above all things to spend in quiet the evening of a laborious life, to get, by admission into smart society and first-rate Pall Mall clubs, the flattering equivalent for the money he was lavishing on the *Whitechapel Wonder* and on other stepping-stones to fashionable consideration. He had indeed been balloted into the Carlton. He found it really less to his liking than those resorts which were at his disposal without an entrance-fee. As for society, he was nowhere; if he entered a Mayfair drawing-room it was only to be called to account by someone who thought himself or herself covertly attacked or satirized in "that accursed newspaper," as Knapp now irritably began to call his broadsheet.

Miss Cherubina Willoughby had not either been as pleasant as usual. When

Knapp placed a cigarette between her lips, and was proceeding to seal the gift, the lady, in decidedly unecclesiastical language, wanted to know how it was that the arts and accomplishments of the "Variety's" artiste were so often unrecognized, while Miss Maud Mammoth's performances in Shakespearean drama were so preposterously overpraised.

IV.

NATHANIEL KNAPP'S COUP D'ETAT

Meanwhile Brabazon and Caroll, with all the young gentlemen, as fresh to newspaper work as themselves, whom they employed, were having a merry time of it. It was not journalism, but it was a capital

s

joke. No weekly dinners of a comic paper can ever have witnessed such screams of laughter at the diners' own esoteric fun as punctuated the editorial labours of Messrs. Caroll, Brabazon, and their staff. Great as was the contrast between the two editors in the Salisbury Street office, they were perfectly at one in resolving to make all which was to be made out of the colonial plutocrat.

How long this golden season might have lasted but for the effect of the already-named considerations on the proprietor of the *Whitechapel Wonder*, it is impossible to say.

At last Nathaniel Knapp took a resolution, and proceeded to carry it out with no word of warning. Going to the newspaper office one day at the hour at which he judged his editors' labours would be over, he was told by the housekeeper, who at first did not recognize him, that

Mr. Caroll was particularly engaged at that moment, and could see no one in his room.

Knapp's temper was up. He was not going to be kept out of his own office. He brushed past the woman, and, walking upstairs, heard a noise as of vocal music in the French tongue issuing, as he thought, from the direction of the editorial sanctum.

A little vestibule was at the top of the stairs. Into it Knapp walked, to find a litter of luncheon dishes and half-consumed dainties in process of removal. The door of the editors' room was ajar. Knapp now knew the owner of the voice to be the person he had suspected. He identified beyond doubt the clear, musical organ of his friend "the clergyman," musically trilling forth a humorous Parisian song, often sung in happier days for his own pleasure.

He looked through the half-open door. There at a table covered with the remains of divers good things sat the proprietress of the bewitching voice, not at this moment singing, but drolly twisting her pretty mouth, nostrils, and eyebrows, as if in imitation of another countenance, into shapes not their own.

Knapp felt as if he should have an apoplexy. While he examined for any signs of seizure his reflection in a looking-glass, it struck him that the imitation which Miss Cherubina Willoughby was giving in the next room must be that of his own proprietorial self. This, indeed, was the case. Knapp hurried off to the office of his solicitor, close by. That gentleman, in execution of his principal's *coup d'état*, intimated to Mr. Caroll that he had ceased to be editor of the *Whitechapel Wonder*, and that his services would not in any other capacity be required.

Nathaniel Knapp, having satiated his appetite for uncouth and sensational titles, resumed for his property its earlier style of *The Mayfair Butterfly;* re-engaged as his editor, not any brilliant amateur of the West End, but the steady-going, sure-footed, serious Mr. Bourgeois, who had been weaned on printers' ink, tucked up in proof-sheets, and who had only in all his life passed three weeks consecutively to the west of Temple Bar.

The *Mayfair Butterfly* flourishes to this day as a highly respectable and perfectly innocent society journal. As for Miss Cherubina Willoughby, Knapp did the handsome thing by the lady—settled upon her a comfortable sum. She shortly afterwards married the heir to a dukedom.

Nathaniel Knapp gave up his chambers in the Albany, found an exemplary wife in a lady of title, the daughter of an earl, has long since got a safe seat in the House of Commons, occupies one of the best Cubitt-built houses in Grosvenor Square, and has never since dabbled in journalism, whether new or old.

The Strange Adventures
of a Sermon

A MAY MEETING'S TALE

I.

BISHOP PINDAR'S MISSION

"IF your mother falls sick, cable to me, c/o General Donald, 666, Westbourne Terrace, Hyde Park, London. Be careful, and avoid even all appearance of evil. You neither drink nor smoke yourself, but yesterday you were with those who do both."

Such were the last words spoken to his son by Bishop Pindar, of Louisiana, before leaving his American home to cross the Atlantic on a temperance oratorical tour in England, beginning in London. In the States, since the days of J. B. Gough, no

Rechabite rhetoric had produced the effect of the Bishop's. In all respects he presented a complete contrast to his predecessor. Like several other good and brave men of his Church, Pindar had worn the sword before he donned the surplice. He had been on Grant's staff during the Civil War ; he had perhaps caught from his chief the calm composure of manner which no surprise or danger could ruffle. His speech was full of emphasis without vehemence. Much of the secret of his influence came from the passionless gravity of his most solemn appeals. The success attending the American revivalists in England, and the accounts which he had heard from them of the drink evil in the furthest and nautical east of London, had much to do with his present expedition.

General Donald, who was to be the Bishop's English host, was a man cast in the same mould as the Havelocks and

Lawrences, who have made our Indian
empire, and who, though brave and loyal
servants of "John Company," or of the
Crown, as the case might be, have gloried
in being first, and above all, soldiers of
the Cross. As a youth, in his native land,
he had distinguished himself in the classes
and examinations of his university; throughout life he had been a hard student as well
as a dauntless fighter. On his final return
to Europe, the seat of learning that had
trained him wished to elect him as its
principal. He declined the honour, but
did eventually consent to contest with a
Cabinet minister the succession to the Lord
Rectorship. In that competition the General
gained unprecedented majorities in all the
nations. The truth is that Donald, while
subordinating his whole life to his idea of
social and religious duty, was yet a practical
man of the world, who did not feel it part
of his creed to forsake the club for the

cloister.   He had been an original member
of the old Oriental Club in Hanover Square;
he still belonged to the Rag; he was on the
committee of the East India United Club,
next door to it.   He was, on the surface,
of an easy and pleasant manner.   Once or
twice some younger men at his clubs, who
knew him well, ventured to rally him on
his Evangelical enthusiasm, and to ask him
whether it was true that at the National
Club in Whitehall, to which he also belonged, he read family prayers every day
with the servants, and preached on Sundays.
The tone of the General's perfectly cour-
teous rejoinder was not such as to provoke
a repetition of the bantering inquiry.

Mrs. General Donald, though an excellent
lady in her way, was not an enthusiast like
her husband in the causes that he considered
good.   Sometimes, it must be admitted, she
found a handle for her jokes against the
General on his undiscriminating sympathies

and hospitalities. For this sturdy soldier was not an infallible judge of the motives and the conduct of all with whom he thought it his duty to co-operate.

"And now this American bishop!" the lady had said. "I hope he is not like the teetotal butler you heard of at the National Club, and who got delirium tremens before the keys of the cellar had been a week in his pocket."

"I hope devoutly not," murmured to himself the General, who was acutely conscious of the opportunity which his mistakes had given the enemy to blaspheme. But audibly he said nothing, and only entreated his wife to see that the same marks of outer respect were paid to the expected guest as if he had been one of the English spiritual lords.

II.

THE GENERAL'S NAP DISTURBED

There's no call to go 'my lord'-ing him like that! He's only a colonial, or something of that sort, and does not rank with an English rector."

So spoke to one of the housemaids at 666, Westbourne Terrace, the butler, Dawley. For in the basement of that house the opinions entertained and expressed reflected rather those of Mrs. Donald than of the General upstairs. Like the shrewd observer which in all things habitually he was, General Donald had noticed one or two real or imaginary failures on the part of his domestics of proper deference towards his guest. The few words of gentle caution addressed by him to his servants on the subject did not tend to increase the visitor's popularity below stairs.

It must have been nearly a week after Bishop Pindar's arrival that, the guest having gone out on business of his own, the host, glad of a quiet day to make up his arrears of reading, writing, of study generally, and of meditation, was sitting in his library, a nobly furnished room, in which the fragrance of Russia leather bindings mingled with that of Persian ivory chessmen in their sandalwood board and case. A little tired with his morning's constitutional, and ready to refresh himself with a siesta for his afternoon's work, the General was not too well pleased when, contrary to the rules of his household, the servant interrupted him with, "A man waiting, waiting in the hall to see you, sir!"

The old soldier checked any rising words of irritation, quieted himself with a strong pull at his moustache, and merely said:

"Tell him the hour to call is 11 a.m. to-morrow, and to write for an appointment."

Thus much, it seemed as a fact, the well-drilled butler had already conveyed to the caller, who, it seems, replied that he came a long way from the other side of London, and that he had something which he must place in the hands of Bishop Pindar, or at least see safely lodged with that ecclesiastic's host.

"What sort of a man, Dawley?" asked the General.

"Looks a seafaring sort of a man, I should say, regular East Ender in dress. Tells me he has come from the 'Spotted Dog,' down East Ham way, with some of the Bishop's property."

"In that case, as his lordship is out, and the man has had a long walk, you had better show him in."

III.

THE LANDLORD OF THE "SPOTTED DOG"

The first effect of the entrance of the stranger, whose bronzed complexion and coarse pea-jacket did not belie Dawley's description of him, was faintly to qualify the Russia leather and sandalwood aroma of General Donald's library with a dash of the scent exhaled by "Negro Head" tobacco, and possibly Jamaica rum. Such odours, at any rate, had before now suffused his garments, and still faintly clung to them. The man's manner was perfectly respectful. Pulling his forelock, he explained himself to be the proprietor of a little tavern generally known as the "Spotted Dog," on the Epping road, and that there had been left on his premises a packet with instructions for it to be returned to Bishop Pindar, c/o General Donald, 666, Westbourne Terrace.

" No offence, sir," the man continued, " but I should like myself to place it in the Bishop's hands."

" The——" The General's lips shaped themselves as if to emit a D-sound, which might have been followed by the words " you would." But, pulling his moustache with subdued fierceness, he stifled the ejaculation of his unregenerate days, and simply said, " The Bishop will be in presently. I will be responsible for the packet, and give it him myself."

Still the landlord of the " Spotted Dog," down Stratford way, delayed. His motive in doing so was obvious enough to the Scotchman who confronted him, and whose Evangelicalism had not taken away his native shrewdness. The publican, of course, as General Donald saw, recognized the compromising nature of the appearances, and wished to make what capital he could out of them for himself. "Surely," so had run the publican's thoughts, "even a missionary, or at least not an English bishop, might be good for a gold coin at the least as compensation for the trouble of restoring the lost property," to say nothing of other aspects of the untoward predicament.

He of the "Spotted Dog" placed upon the table the packet, just sufficiently open for the General to read the inscription : "To be returned to Bishop Pindar, etc., immediately." There could be no doubt as to what the article in question was. It could not be anything else but a sermon, lecture, or homily of some sort, divested of the outer silk covering which usually encases such discourses.

General Donald, though a stranger to fear upon ordinary occasions, was conscious of his looks betraying his internal discomfort ; he was indeed perplexed and

T

vexed more than he could have found
words to express. Had he once more been
deceived by appearances? As his wife
had ventured to hint, and the servants
below stairs firmly believed, was his episcopal guest a scamp in disguise? Had the
General himself become once more the dupe
of an unscrupulous adventurer, as but some
months ago he had been of a so-called
revivalist from foreign parts, who turned
out to be much wanted by the police of
two continents?

While he revolved these things in his
mind, a cab stopped at his door; the next
moment Bishop Pindar was in the room.
Entering apparently in a state of some
agitation, the prelate was not restored to
composure by the expression on his host's
face. Amid his nervous preoccupation, he
disregarded the presence of the East End
publican, but, standing near to General
Donald's table, caught a glimpse of a

familiar and much-missed document. With
the words " My sermon restored, I declare ! "
the prelate made as though he would have
put the document in his pocket. But at
this moment a knock at the front door was
heard. Presently a servant entered, with
the card of " Mr. Ronald Macpherson," of
the *Daily Courier*, who desired at once,
though only for a moment, to see Bishop
Pindar, or, if he were out, General Donald.

IV.

THE MYSTERY CLEARED UP

What had really happened requires now,
with the briefest possible retrospect, to
be explained. Among the objects dear
to the heart of the good American Bishop
was the rescue from the temptations there
besetting them of sailors of all nations

in the densely populated shipping districts
near to the London Victoria Docks. He
had lived and laboured among this sort
of men in his native New Orleans; he
knew them thoroughly. Of invincible
faith, not in himself, but in a higher aid
which he had never found fail him, he
felt that he had a mission to all Eng-
lish-speaking seafaring folk, to whichever
branch of the Anglo - Saxon race they
belonged. Therefore, instead of preaching
on Sunday at St. Paul's, whose pulpit had
been placed at his disposal, the Bishop
decided to deliver his address in a huge
building between East and West Ham, that
very quarter near to which, though before
whose existence by that name, once ran the
high - road from London to the eastern
counties.

The *Daily Courier* was the chief organ
of the philanthropic public. Special reports
of all that was said or done for the good

of those who could not help themselves
constituted a special feature in its columns.
The most capable stenographers of its staff
were always told off for such occasions.
Than Ronald Macpherson, like others, the
flower of his order, an Aberdonian, the *Daily
Courier* and all Fleet Street could show
no better shorthand writer. Bishop Pindar's
East End address being a feature of the
spring meeting season, was entrusted to
this Scotch expert to report. Parliament
was of course at the same time in session
at Westminster. With the Law Courts in
the morning, and the Houses at night, a
stronger man even than Macpherson might
well have been exhausted at the week's end.
Such indeed was his fatigue that during
the first part of the Saturday night he
tossed feverishly in his bed from side to
side without closing his eyes. At last a
dull, heavy sleep came. When Macpherson
awoke to consciousness, the Sunday bells

were ringing. The reporter remembered
he was due for Bishop Pindar's address in
the Ham Tabernacle. A sharp stroke of
inward agony seemed to run a red - hot
dagger through him. His Scotch self-
possession came to his rescue; in ten
minutes he was driving as fast as hansom
cab could fly from his home in Brixton,
where so many gentlemen of his craft
dwell, to the densely populated district some
two or three miles off. As Macpherson
knew must be the case, the function in the
Ham Hall was finished before he reached
the place. But—and he devoutly thanked
Heaven that it was so—Bishop Pindar was
still on the premises. It was not a work
of many minutes to find that divine, personally to explain to him what had
happened, and how his timely aid alone
could enable the overworked reporter to
save his reputation with his employers, and
to provide the printer of the *Daily Courier*

for the following Monday that same evening with the "copy" for the report of the Bishop's address.

Before Pindar entrusted the document to the stenographer he remembered to write on the outside sheet of it in bold characters the address, the construction of which the reader already knows. The Fleet Street offices of London daily newspapers do not open to their staff till some hours after noon. Nor even in the best-regulated of them on the first day of the week is there always good accommodation for writing until the evening, when the printers are actually at work.

Macpherson was naturally anxious to get back to his Brixton home, so that he might eat his afternoon dinner with his family on the one day in the week which he could call his own. The only possibility of his doing this was for him to copy out the Bishop's address while he was yet in

the Ham district, and thence despatch it
to the office of his newspaper.   Macpherson
knew even less of metropolitan places of
entertainment than did most of his careful
and frugal colleagues.   He had, however,
heard of a tavern locally styled the " Spotted
Dog," not very far from the site of the
historic thoroughfare already mentioned, in
old days a house of some repute.   From
hearsay he felt himself sure here of finding
a quiet corner in which he could copy out
the episcopal manuscript.

" Nothing   stronger   than   a   big   pot   of
your best tea, with a few slices of bread-
and - butter."   Such   were   Macpherson's   instructions as he passed through the bar to
the little room allotted him upstairs for his
work.

Our stenographer was a quick longhand
writer.   In little more than an hour his
task was done, ready for the printer ; he
was free to rejoin his family in Brixton.

Passing through the bar-parlour, or bar itself, he just stopped to give his host "Good-day," and to pay the little bill. A Presbyterian by nurture, it was with the agitation of a guilty man that he prepared to issue forth into the street.

On his way home he took the office of his newspaper. Putting his hand in his pocket, he found his own manuscript safe there, but did not at once feel or miss or even think of the Bishop's manuscript. He had gone too far now on his way home with any good result to turn back. Bishop Pindar's sermon-case would be safe in the room where its transcription for the newspaper had been done. So, tolerably at ease, he returned to his suburban home just in time for the Sunday joint. As he hoped in time enough to prevent complications, on the Monday he repaired to the inn where he had worked on the previous day.

Meanwhile the landlord of this place, ignorant of his Sunday customer, and seeing in the document left on his premises the potentiality of a small windfall in cash, had, as the reader knows, called at General Donald's, in Westbourne Terrace.

Directly Macpherson possessed himself of this fact, shrewdly discerning the elements of a compromising situation for the Bishop, he followed in a cab, and now, in the presence of the General, the prelate, and the publican, gave substantially the same version of the facts as has been set forth here.

" It seemed, certainly, a strange place for the sermon-book of an episcopal temperance preacher." So commented on the facts General Donald, not without a secret sigh of relief that his wife would not, as a short time ago it seemed certain she would, have another story against him for her non-Evangelical and society friends.

As for the "Spotted Dog," it will be looked for to-day in vain, for it has long since been turned into a tea and coffee tavern. Its landlord humbly follows in Bishop Pindar's preaching wake.

PLYMOUTH
WILLIAM BRENDON AND SON
PRINTERS

BOOKS TO READ ——

AND

—— BOOKS TO BUY.

GREENING & CO.'s
NEW AND FORTHCOMING
PUBLICATIONS.

A Trip to Paradoxia, and other Humours of the Hour. Being Contemporary Pictures of Social Fact and Political Fiction. A Work of Social Satire by T. H. S. ESCOTT, Author of "Personal Forces of the Period," "Social Transformation of the Victorian Age," "Platform, Press, Politics and Play," etc. Cover designed by W. S. ROGERS. *Crown 8vo, art cloth, gilt.* **5/- nett.**

The Lady of the Leopard. A Powerful and Fascinating Novel by CHAS. L'EPINE, Author of "The Devil in a Domino." Cover designed by W. S. ROGERS. *Crown 8vo, art cloth.* **3/6**

The Sword of Fate. An Interesting Novel by HENRY HERMAN, Author of "Eagle Joe," "Scarlet Fortune," etc., and Joint Author of "The Silver King," "Claudian," etc. Cover designed by W. S. ROGERS. *Crown 8vo, art cloth.* **3/6**

The Hypocrite. A Realistic Novel of Oxford and London Life. Third Impression. Cover designed by SCOTSON CLARKE. *Crown 8vo, cloth.* **2/6**

Darab's Wine-Cup, and other Powerful and Vividly- Written Stories by BART KENNEDY, Author of "The Wandering Romanoff," etc. Cover designed by W. S. ROGERS. *Crown 8vo, cloth.* **2/6**

Bye-Ways of Crime, being the Story of the Black
Museum, its Histories and Mystery, by R. J. POWER-BERREY.
Profusely illustrated. *Crown 8vo, cloth.* 3/6

The Resurrection of His Grace. A Sporting Novel
by CAMPBELL RAE-BROWN, Author of "Richard Barlow,"
"Kissing Cup's Race," etc. Cover designed by W. S. ROGERS.
Crown 8vo, cloth, gilt. 2/6

My Lady Ruby; and **Basileon: Chief of Police.**
Two Stories by G. F. MONKSHOOD, Author of "Nightshades."
Crown 8vo, art cloth. 2/6

Such is the Law! A Novel by MARIE M. SADLIER,
Author of "Lightest London," "An Uncanny Girl," etc. *Crown
8vo, cloth.* 6/-

Seven Nights with Satan. A Novel by J. L. OWEN,
Author of "The Great Jekyll Diamond." Cover designed by
W. S. ROGERS. *Crown 8vo, cloth.* 3/6

The Pottle Papers. A Really Funny Book, written by
SAUL SMIFF, and Illustrated by L. RAVEN HILL. Third
Impression. *Crown 8vo, art cloth, top edge gilt.* 2/6

A Social Upheaval. An Unconventional Satirical Novel,
by ISIDORE G. ASCHER. *Crown 8vo, cloth extra.* 6/-

The Green Passion. The Study of a Jealous Soul.
A Powerful Novel by ANTHONY P. VERT. Cover designed by
ALFRED PRAGA. *Crown 8vo, art cloth.* 3/6

Dan Leno, Hys Booke. A Volume of Frivolities:
Autobiographical, Historical, Philosophical, Anecdotal and Non-
sensical. Written by DAN LENO. Illustrated by S. H. SIME,
FRANK CHESWORTH, W. S. ROGERS, GUSTAVE DARRE,
ALFRED BRYAN and DAN LENO. Fourth Edition contains an
Appreciation of Dan Leno, written by CLEMENT SCOTT. *Crown
8vo, art cloth, gilt edges.* 2/-
Sewed, illustrated wrapper 1/-

In Quaint East Anglia. Descriptive Sketches by
T. WEST CARNIE. Illustrated. *Long 12mo, cloth.* 1/-

Shadows; or, Glimpses of Society. By ERNEST DE
P. MARTIN. *Crown 8vo, art cloth.* 2/6

The Gates of Temptation. A Natural Novel by
Mrs. ALBERT S. BRADSHAW, Author of "False Gods," "Wife
or Slave," etc. *Crown 8vo, cloth.* 2/6

"Fame, the Fiddler." A Literary and Theatrical
Novel by S. J. ADAIR FITZ-GERALD. *Crown 8vo, cloth, new
and cheaper Edition.* 2/6

Madonna Mia, and other Stories by CLEMENT SCOTT.
Cover designed by W. S. ROGERS. *Crown 8vo, cloth.* 3/6

The Wheel of Life. A Few Memories and Recollections (de omnibus rebus) by CLEMENT SCOTT. With Portrait of
the Author from the celebrated Painting by J. MORDECAI. Third
Edition. *Crown 8vo, crimson buckram, gilt lettered, gilt top.* 2/-
POPULAR EDITION, *paper cover.* 6d.

"Sisters by the Sea." Seaside and Country Sketches,
by CLEMENT SCOTT. Frontispiece and Vignette designed by
GEO. POWNALL. Third Edition. *Long 12mo, attractively
bound in cloth.* 1/-

Four Famous Hamlets. (Henry Irving, Beerbohm
Tree, Wilson Barrett, and Forbes Robertson.) By CLEMENT
SCOTT. Illustrated. *Crown 8vo, cloth.* (*In preparation*) 2/6

The Grand Panjandrum. Fairy Tales for Children,
by S. J. ADAIR FITZ-GERALD. Full-page and other Illustrations
by GUSTAVE DARRE. *Square 8vo, fancy cloth.* 3/6

Lord Jimmy. A Story of Music-Hall Life by GEORGE
MARTYN. *Crown 8vo, cloth.* 2/6

The Lady of Criswold. A Sensational Story by
LEONARD OUTRAM. *Crown 8vo, cloth.* 2/6

Doña Rufina. A Nineteenth Century Romance. Being
a Story of Carlist Conspiracy by HEBER DANIELS, Author of
"Our Tenants." *Crown 8vo, cloth.* 2/6

The Art of Elocution and Public Speaking. By
ROSS FERGUSON, with an Introduction by GEORGE ALEXANDER.
Dedicated by permission to Miss ELLEN TERRY. *Crown 8vo,
strongly bound in cloth.* 1/-

Death and the Woman. A Powerful Tale by ARNOLD GOLSWORTHY. Picture Cover drawn by SYDNEY H. SIME. *Crown 8vo.* **1/-**

The Devil in a Domino. A Psychological Mystery by CHAS. L'EPINE, Author of "The Lady of the Leopard," "Miracle Plays," etc. Cover designed by C. H. BEAUVAIS. *Long 12mo, sewed.* **6d.** *Cloth Edition.* **1/-**

That Fascinating Widow, and other Frivolous and Fantastic Tales, for River, Road, and Rail, by S. J. ADAIR FITZ-GERALD. *Long 12mo, sewed.* **6d.** *Cloth Edition.* **1/-**

The Fellow-Passengers. A Mystery and its Solution. A Detective Story by RIVINGTON PIKE, Author of "The Man who Disappeared." *Long 12mo, sewed.* **6d.** *Cloth Edition.* **1/-**

London. A Handy Guide for the Visitor, Sportsman, and Naturalist by J. W. CUNDALL. Numerous Illustrations. Second Year of Publication. *Long 12mo, cloth.* **6d.**

America Abroad. A Handy Guide for Americans in England. Edited by J. W. CUNDALL. With numerous Illustrations. Ninth Year of Publication. **6d.** *Cloth Edition.* **1/-**

Miss Malevolent. A Realistic Study, by the Author of "The Hypocrite." *Crown 8vo, art cloth.* (*In active preparation*) **2/6**

Rudyard Kipling. An Appreciation by G. F. MONKS-HOOD. Containing two letters by Rudyard Kipling, and a portrait. *Crown 8vo, buckram, gilt top.* **5/-**

Yule-Tide Tales. A Volume of Dramatic and Humorous Stories, by CLEMENT SCOTT, S. J. ADAIR FITZ-GERALD, Mrs. ALBERT S. BRADSHAW, T. C. ELDER, GEORGES JACOBI, W. SCOTT FOLKESTONE, A. DEWAR WILLOCH, HARRY MONK-HOUSE, ARTHUR COLLINS, HORACE LENNARD, GEO. ALEX-ANDER, ROSS FERGUSON, GEO. POWNALL, DAN LENO, etc. Numerous full-page Pictures and other smaller Illustrations (including Portraits of Contributors) by SYDNEY H. SIME, ALICK RITCHIE, EDWARD READE, BERNARD MUNNS, CLAUDE CALTHORPE, etc. *4to, fancy wrapper.* **6d.**

The Shadow on the Manse. A Novel by CAMPBELL RAE-BROWN. *Crown 8vo, cloth.* **3/6**

The Pillypingle Pastorals. A New Humorous Book by DRUID GRAYLE. Illustrated by WALTER J. MORGAN, R.B.A. *Crown 8vo, cloth.* (*In preparation*) **3/6**

The Dolomite Cave. An Exciting Tale of Adventure by W. PATRICK KELLY, Author of "Schoolboys Three," etc. *Crown 8vo, cloth.* (*In preparation*) **6/-**

An Amateur Fiend. A Pathetic Humorous Story by SAUL SMIFF, Author of "The Pottle Papers." Illustrated by W. S. ROGERS. *Crown 8vo, cloth.* (*In preparation*) **3/6**

Zorastro. A Romance of the Middle Ages. By C. J. S. THOMPSON, Author of "The Mystery and Romance of Alchemy," "Poison Romance and Poison Mysteries," etc. *Crown 8vo, cloth.* (*In preparation*) **3/6**

Dazzled. A Novel of Theatrical Life as it really is, by a New Writer. *Crown 8vo, cloth.* (*In preparation*) **6/-**

Fetters of Fire. A Powerful Novel by COMPTON READE. Author of "Hard Lines," "Under which King," etc. *Crown 8vo, cloth.* (*In preparation*) **6/-**

Ashes Tell no Tales. An Interesting Novel by Mrs. ALBERT S. BRADSHAW, Author of "The Gates of Temptation," "False Gods," etc. *Crown 8vo, cloth.* (*In preparation*) **6/-**

The Pottle's Progress. A New Humorous Book by SAUL SMIFF, Author of "The Pottle Papers," "An Amateur Fiend," etc. *Crown 8vo, art cloth.* (*In preparation*) **2/6**

People, Plays, and Places. Being the Second Series of *The Wheel of Life*, Memories and Recollections of *People* I have met, *Plays* I have seen, and *Places* I have visited, by CLEMENT SCOTT, Author of "Madonna Mia," "The Stage of Yesterday and The Stage of To-day," "Sisters by the Sea," "Pictures of the World," "Poppyland," etc. *Crown 8vo, cloth gilt.* (*In preparation*) **5/-**

GREENING & CO.,
20, Cecil Court, Charing Cross Road, LONDON, W.C.

www.ingramcontent.com/pod-product-compliance
Lightning Source LLC
Chambersburg PA
CBHW031401270326
41929CB00010BA/1286